GUIDANCE HANDBOOK
FOR
SECONDARY SCHOOLS

Prepared by

DIVISION OF RESEARCH AND GUIDANCE
With the Assistance of
Division of Trade and Industrial Education
Division of Secondary Education
Division of Health and Physical Education
Division of Audio-Visual Education
Division of Attendance and Child Welfare

of the

OFFICE OF LOS ANGELES COUNTY SUPERINTENDENT
OF SCHOOLS

COUNTY BOARD OF EDUCATION
Drummond J. McCunn, President
Claude L. Reeves, Vice President
Mrs. Ruth Darsie, Member
William A. Sheldon, Member
C. C. Trillingham, County Superintendent
of Schools, and Ex Officio Secretary

Los Angeles County, California

ꝏ

Los Angeles
CALIFORNIA TEST BUREAU
1948

Authors
Guidance Handbook for Secondary Schools

Dr. Harry Smallenburg, Director, Division of Research and Guidance.

Mr. Lee W. Ralston, Director, Division of Trade and Industrial Education.

Mrs. Esther Grace Nolan, Secondary Research and Guidance Coordinator.

Dr. Emery Stoops, formerly Secondary Research and Guidance Coordinator; now Administrative Assistant.

Dr. Arthur T. Tait, formerly Educational Statistician; now Assistant Director of Research, California Test Bureau.

Mr. Claude E. Wilson, Secondary Research and Guidance Coordinator.

Printed in the United States of America

All royalties received from the sale of this Handbook are paid directly to the Los Angeles County School Service Fund.

First Printing March 1948
Second Printing January 1949

For sale by the California Test Bureau
5916 Hollywood Boulevard, Los Angeles 28, California

FOREWORD

The results of careful planning and discussion on the part of representatives of all Divisions in the Office of the County Superintendent of Schools directly concerned with secondary education are embodied in this handbook. However, the chief responsibility for the actual preparation rested upon the professional staff members of the Division of Research and Guidance.

The handbook is designed for use by all educators in Los Angeles County secondary schools who share in the responsibility for guidance of students. Naturally much of the content is designed for teachers and counselors who work directly with students. Suggestions for the organization and administration of a guidance program of special value to superintendents and principals are included.

The chief emphasis is on techniques, which run the gamut from standardized testing through observation, the interview, the questionnaire, and the case study, to evaluation of the guidance program itself. The list of modern guidance materials including basic references for guidance workers, should be of considerable value.

The best modern research and practice have been drawn upon in the preparation of this handbook. We believe that the techniques suggested are basically sound and eminently practical. Yet we do not look on the handbook as being either complete or final. Suggestions from school people of the county and from other persons interested in improving the guidance of secondary school students will be received gratefully.

It is hoped that this handbook will be of material aid to all teachers, counselors, and administrators in the secondary schools of Los Angeles County in furnishing needed guidance to their students.

C. C. TRILLINGHAM
County Superintendent of Schools.

whole field of guidance by a careful perusal of this volume. Specialists in guidance can use it as a handbook in their own specialized tasks and in furnishing guidance leadership to the entire school faculty. Lay people—P. T. A. members, Coordinating Council members, and just plain citizens interested in schools and school procedure—may be helped in their understanding of community and home problems by the clear cut principles and techniques set forth in this handbook.

5. Point of View.

The point of view is eclectic and modern. No one given technique is set up as the answer for the guidance problems of youth. The old stand-by of standardized testing is not deserted. Newer methods, such as observation of students and recording data concerning them and the case study technique are given their just due. The fact that modern, scientific guidance must rest on a sound basis of objective data is taken for granted. Adequate cumulative records are assumed to form an integral part of the guidance program. Inclusion of practically all of the leading guidance techniques which have been found helpful at the secondary school level adds comprehensiveness to the merits of this compendium.

6. Emphasis.

Emphasis is placed in the very beginning of the handbook on the essential characteristics of a guidance program. Included among those essentials are definite purposes, appropriate organization, suitable administrative arrangements, various guidance techniques, in-service growth of staff members in guidance, interpretation of the guidance program to the community, and finally, evaluation of the guidance program itself.

The great importance of the role of administrators in connection with the success of guidance programs is indicated in Chapter III by the following phases of guidance for which administrators are responsible:

(1) Development of a guidance philosophy in cooperation with their staff.

(2) Assignment of responsibility for planning and administering a guidance program.

(3) Cooperative consideration of problems in developing and operating a guidance program.

(4) Provision of adequate facilities for guidance.

(5) Utilization of available County and State resources.

(6) Support of and continuous interest in the guidance program.

7. Organization and Content.

The whole subject of guidance in the secondary school is introduced by referring to social problems which affect education, and to purposes of education. These references are supplemented by the listing of characteristics and needs of boys and girls and essential characteristics of a guidance program.

Techniques for collecting and recording guidance data including the testing program, the interview, observation and recording of student behavior, the autobiography, the questionnaire, the case study, and the cumulative record system are explained. The use of guidance data by administrators for promotion and special placement and for the improvement of curricular offerings is suggested.

Group guidance techniques, such as core curriculum and guidance classes, special classes, extra-currilar activities, and special guidance events are presented. Techniques for the use of teachers and counselors in giving students educational and vocational guidance and in guiding them regarding physical and mental health and personal-social problems are elaborated. The counseling process is also discussed.

Techniques for improving professional growth in guidance, for interpreting the guidance program to the public generally and for appraising the guidance program are also given considerable attention.

Modern guidance materials including differentiated reading materials for students, audio-visual aids, materials on occupational information, and basic references for guidance workers are listed at some length.

8. Special Features.

Special features comprise the following: (1) Los Angeles County Promotional Policy, (2) suggested use of guidance data for improving curricular offerings, (3) a personal questionnaire form, and (4) a check list of guidance services.

The promotional policy for secondary schools is similar to the promotional policy for elementary schools which was first promulgated in 1940. It involves adjustment of the educational program to the interests and needs of secondary school students so that a limited amount of acceleration or retardation for any given student results.

The use of guidance data to improve curricular offerings is discussed but is not treated extensively in this book. Elaboration of this theme probably belongs in a treatise in the curriculum field. However, this recognition of the importance of using guidance data for curricular improvements should serve as an incentive to further effort along that line.

A suggested personal questionnaire for secondary school use is included in the chapter on Techniques for Collecting and Recording Guidance Data. This form calls for considerable information concerning the home and family, school activities, vocational plans, leisure time, and so forth. This form or an adaptation of it could be used to advantage in any secondary school in connection with the guidance of all students.

The check list of guidance services in Chapter IX is an approach to the difficult problem of appraisal of the guidance program. This can be used to appraise the program in an individual school or in all the secondary schools of a school system. Provision is made on the list for indicating different degrees of service ranging from "not at all" to "very great." Comprehensive coverage of the entire guidance program, as set forth in the handbook, is afforded by this list.

9. **References and Materials in the Appendix.**

The suggested references at the end of chapters, or chapter sections, have been chosen carefully with a view to giving specific help in the further study of problems treated in those chapters or sections.

Basic references for guidance workers, which are listed at the end of Chapter VI, are intended to help teachers, counselors, and administrators with their common guidance problems. All of these books should be readily available to every secondary school faculty.

The selected references on guidance at the end of the book include books, periodical articles, year-books and monographs, publications of the County Superintendent of Schools Office, U. S. Government publications, and special materials.

Included in the appendix are useful materials such as charts showing different types of organization for guidance, a list of available tests, a list of publishing companies referred to in the handbook, County Office Bulletins relative to testing, and County Office forms.

10. Supplementing the Handbook.

Inasmuch as the material in this handbook represents a brief outline only of the field of secondary school guidance, it is definitely realized that it must be supplemented by other materials to be of maximum value in planning and conducting a guidance program. Part of this supplementation can be achieved through the use of references listed at various places throughout the handbook. Other supplementary materials in the form of bulletins and forms especially adapted to guidance programs in high schools of the County will be issued from time to time as the need for such materials arises.

R. B. WALTER
Chief Deputy Superintendent.

ACKNOWLEDGMENTS.

The following members of the staff of the Division of Research and Guidance carried heavy responsibilities in preparing the Handbook in its final form:

Mrs. Esther Grace Nolan, Coordinator of Research and Guidance, Secondary.

Dr. Emery Stoops, formerly Coordinator of Research and Guidance, Secondary; now, Administrative Assistant to the County Superintendent of Schools.

Dr. Arthur T. Tait, Educational Statistician.

Mr. Claude Wilson, Coordinator of Research and Guidance, Secondary.

Special acknowledgment should also be made of the services of Mr. Lee W. Ralston, Director, Division of Trade and Industrial Education, Los Angeles County Schools, who served as conference leader in the development of major portions of the Handbook.

Representatives of other divisions who made important contributions related to their special responsibilities and interests include:

Dr. Reuben Palm, Director, Division of Secondary Education.

Mr. Ernest Toland, Secondary Curriculum Coordinator.

Mrs. Helen Rachford, Director, Division of Audio-Visual Education.

Mr. Lloyd Webster, Director, Division of Health and Physical Education.

Mr. John R. Hunt, Director, Division of Attendance and Child Welfare.

Dr. H. B. McDaniel met several times with the group while he was serving as Chief of the Division of Occupational Information and Guidance, California State Department of Education, and made many significant suggestions.

Special acknowledgments are also due Dr. Willis W. Clark, former Director of the Division of Research and Guidance,

Los Angeles County Schools, for leadership in developing guidance policies and procedures during his period of service.

The diligent and conscientious efforts of the following secretaries were invaluable in the development of handbook materials: Miss Alma Jaekel, Mrs. Elzanore Gruwell, Miss Annette Bayzerman, Miss Haruko Tatsumi, Miss Sarah Lepp, Miss Anne Lepp and Mrs. Eleanor Cook.

A preliminary edition of the Handbook was used experimentally in summer courses at the University of Southern California, the University of California at Los Angeles, and Stanford University. Acknowledgments are due the students and instructors of these courses for their suggestions and recommendations.

Portions of the Handbook have been reviewed by the Los Angeles County Secondary Guidance Group composed of counselors, teachers and administrators of Los Angeles County high schools.

Members of the Staff of the County Superintendent of Schools who have worked directly on the Handbook acknowledge their indebtedness to Los Angeles County teachers, counselors and administrators, who have made invaluable contributions to guidance through the programs which they have developed for their students. Many of these contributions have been incorporated in the Handbook.

To all who have thus dedicated their time, thought and effort for the benefit of boys and girls in the secondary schools we express sincere appreciation.

HARRY SMALLENBURG,
Director, Division of Research and
Guidance, Los Angeles County
Schools.

TABLE OF CONTENTS

GUIDANCE HANDBOOK FOR SECONDARY SCHOOLS

TABLE OF CONTENTS Continued

TABLE OF CONTENTS Continued

TABLE OF CONTENTS Continued

TABLE OF CONTENTS Continued

TABLE OF CONTENTS Continued

TABLE OF CONTENTS Continued

CHAPTER I

GUIDANCE IN THE MODERN SECONDARY SCHOOL

The modern school has two basic responsibilities: first, to the democratic society which supports it; second, to the boys and girls whom it serves. It is the purpose of this first chapter to discuss briefly the following, in four sections:

Social Problems Which Influence Education.

Purposes of Education in American Democracy.

Characteristics and Needs of Boys and Girls in Secondary Schools.

Essential Characteristics of a Guidance Program Designed to Assist Youth to Participate in Modern Society.

SECTION A. SOCIAL PROBLEMS WHICH INFLUENCE EDUCATION.

The demands of a long-range peace-time economy accentuate the problems of modern society. It is necessary that the secondary school take such problems as the following into account, if it is to assist youth to prepare for intelligent participation in our modern social order:

1. Changes in the role of the home and the family.
2. Shift from rural to urban modes of living.
3. Intermixture of races, nationalities, cultures and creeds.

1

4. Increasing compactness of the world due to improvements in transportation and communication.
5. The lag in adapting social processes to rapid development in science.
6. Emergence of postwar problems including those arising from controlling the new powers of atomic energy.

SECTION B. PURPOSES OF EDUCATION IN AMERICAN DEMOCRACY.

Numerous statements of basic purposes of education have been prepared. One of the most comprehensive and usable of these has been presented by the Educational Policies Commission in the publication, **The Purposes of Education in American Democracy.**

"Four aspects of educational purpose have been identified. These aspects center around the person himself, his relationships to others in home and community, the creation and use of material wealth and socio-civic activities. The first area calls for a description of the educated **person;** the second, for a description of the educated **member of the family and community group;** the third, of the educated **producer or consumer;** the fourth, of the educated **citizen.**

"The four great groups of objectives thus defined are:
1. The Objectives of Self-Realization.
2. The Objectives of Human Relationship.
3. The Objectives of Economic Efficiency.
4. The Objectives of Civic Responsibility.

"Each of these is related to each of the others. Each is capable of further subdivision."[1]

---

[1]Educational Policies Commission, *The Purposes of Education in American Democracy* (Washington, D. C.: National Education Association, 1938), p. 47.

A brief, serviceable statement of long-term objectives has also been adapted from the "Seven Cardinal Principles" by the Subcommittee of the Citizens' Advisory Committee on Readjustment Education of the California Reconstruction and Reemployment Commission. This report, entitled *Postwar Objectives of Public Education in California,*[2] highlights the following basic purposes of education in California:

1. Health.
2. Command of fundamental processes.
3. Vocational preparation.
4. Home membership.
5. Civic education.
6. Character.
7. Use of leisure.

SECTION C. CHARACTERISTICS AND NEEDS OF BOYS AND GIRLS.

1. Adolescence—a period of change.

    Boys and girls in junior and senior high schools range in age from twelve or thirteen to eighteen or nineteen years. Most of them are going through the adolescent period, the stage of growth which lies between childhood with its dependence and parental control, and maturity with its independence and adult responsibility. The adolescent period is one of change; change in body appearance and functions; change in relationships with family and members of the opposite sex; change in relationships with fellow students as well as older groups; change in responsibility for earning a living.

---

[2]California State Reconstruction and Reemployment Commission, "Postwar Objectives of Public Education in California" (Unpublished report, The Commission, Sacramento 14, February, 1945).

2. Physical growth.

The phenomenon of rapid physical growth in adolescence can be understood more clearly if presented in relation to the sequence or pattern of growth from conception through maturity. Although individual variations occur, all human beings follow approximately the same pattern or sequence of growth.[3] The first of the cycles of accelerated growth starts early in the prenatal period and reaches its peak approximately at birth. From birth to the third or fourth year there is a slowing up of the rate of growth. Growth then continues at a fairly uniform rate until the beginning of the puberal cycle. This cycle lasts for a period of from four to seven years. It is followed by an interval of from one to five years during which the rate of growth diminishes.

The changes in velocity of growth of boys from birth to age twenty are shown in Figure 1 following. It will be noted that there is a short but clearly defined retardation in the speed of growth just prior to the onset of the adolescent or puberal cycle. As illustrated in Figure 1, the rate of growth during adolescence is more rapid than at any previous period except in infancy.

[3]Material on growth characteristics of adolescents is based chiefly on the following: Commission on Teacher Education, "Physiological Aspects of Child Growth and Development" (Division on Child Development and Teacher Personnel; Washington, D. C.: American Council on Education, June, 1941).

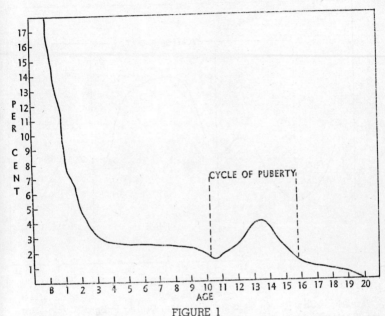

FIGURE 1

Schematic Curve of Changes in Velocity of Growth of Boys from Birth to Twenty Years.[4]   (With permission of Herbert R. Stolz.)

Studies of the physical growth of adolescents consistently show that physical growth occurs in three successive phases, as illustrated in Figure 2.   For the average child the first of these begins immediately after the prepuberal dip at the age of about ten years-six months, and lasts until approximately the middle of the twelfth year.   The second phase extends from about twelve years-eight months to approximately sixteen years.   The third phase extends from sixteen to nearly eighteen years.   The adolescent cycle lasts for a period of approximately four to seven years.   The average duration is about five and one-half years.

[4]Ibid., p. 3.

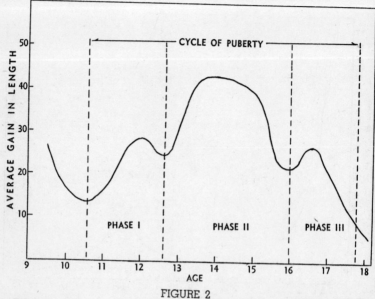

FIGURE 2

Pattern of Changes in Velocity of Growth During Pueral Cycle Showing Three-phase Sequence.[5] (With permission of Herbert R. Stolz.)

Girls enter the cycle of puberty earlier than boys and progress through the various phases of growth at an earlier age. This growth rate is illustrated in Figure 3. It will be noted that, for girls, the period of rapid adolescent growth begins at nine or ten years and continues until fourteen, with a slowing up of the rate of physical change lasting for several more years. On the other hand, the period of rapid adolescent growth in boys begins at approximately ten or eleven years and continues until approximately sixteen, with a gradual decreasing over a several-year period.

Ibid., p. 3.

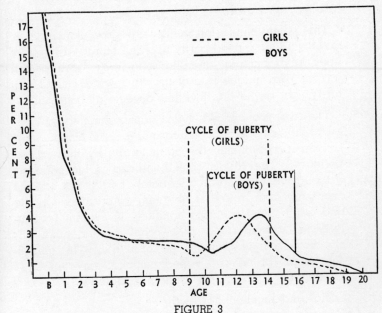

FIGURE 3

Schematic Curves of Changes in Velocity of Growth of Boys and Girls from Birth to Age Twenty.[6] (With permission of Herbert R. Stolz.)

On the average, a girl shows her initial puberal increase in height and weight at approximately eleven years of age and she approaches her maximum stature at the age of fifteen. For the average boy, the initial spurt in height and weight occurs at about age thirteen, and his maximum stature is not reached until after age seventeen. Although it is helpful to consider the average or typical pattern of growth, it is important for the teacher and counselor to remember that **each individual has his own growth curve or pattern** which may differ significantly from the norms shown in the preceding illustrations.

[6]Ibid., p. 4.

3. Intellectual Growth.

The potentialities for intellectual development of a given student depend partly upon hereditary and partly upon environmental or cultural factors. Each person has his own unique rate of growth toward mental maturity, just as he has in other aspects of behavior.

The most pronounced characteristic of increased mental ability is apparent in reasoning. The child learns by direct experience; the adult learns by indirect experience. The child's chief handicap is inexperience. Although he can reason adequately he has not had the necessary background to give him adult understanding and adult interests. This handicap is evident particularly in learning about civic problems and other abstractions remote from his personal life. The adolescent needs broad and varied personal experiences to understand problems in modern society.

4. Social and Emotional Growth.

During the period of early adolescence, boys prefer to participate in activities with members of their own sex. In addition to the normal interest in athletics, they choose such hobbies as gathering collections and airplane construction. Adolescent girls are developing interests in the opposite sex with the accompanying desire to improve their personal appearance through makeup, hair dressing and stylish clothing; and also to improve their human relationships through such activities as parties and dancing.

Approximately two-thirds of the girls in the seventh and eighth grades are in the early stages of adolescence, while an equal number of boys are still pre-adolescent in attitudes and behavior. This difference in age of sex maturation may create behavior problems in the junior high school. In later adolescence these differences between the sexes in social and emotional maturity become less apparent.

5. Individual Differences.

Although there is a similar growth pattern and sequence for all people, each individual follows this pattern at his own rate and in his own way. Hereditary and environmental factors influence each individual's growth in such a way as to make him unique physically, mentally and socially. This may be illustrated by the great psychological differences which exist among the boys and girls in the ordinary classroom. A teacher of the tenth grade, for instance, may expect that in a class of forty students approximately twenty will be of average learning ability; eight or nine will be rapid learners and will perform at a level characteristic of students in the eleventh or twelfth grades. Probably one or two students will be exceptionally intelligent and will be able to reason at an adult level. In the same classroom the teacher may also expect to find six or seven students who are slow-learning and who will perform at an eighth- or ninth-grade level. He may possibly have one or two students who will do school work at a level characteristic of sixth- or seventh-graders.

It is generally recognized that these intellectual differences have important implications for teachers. Equally important are differences in social maturity which result from parental attitudes, economic status and racial or religious background.

6. Needs of Adolescents.

Certain needs are basic to all human beings. Among these are the physical needs of food, rest and activity. These physical drives offer strong motivation to human behavior. Deprivation of them causes serious damage.

Other fundamental needs can be listed as:[7]

a. Need for **affection.** To live in a mutual relationship of warm regard with one or more individuals.

b. Need for **belonging.** To feel that one is an accepted, valued member of a group.

c. Need for **independence.** To be able to make many of one's own decisions and to carry out one's purposes.

d. Need for **social approval.** To feel that one's personality and one's actions are respected and admired by others.

e. Need for maintaining **self-esteem.** To feel that one's conduct comes up to certain inner standards and that it merits one's own respect.

Recognition of these basic needs of all people has been made in the statement of purposes of education presented in Section B of this chapter. The needs of the adolescent are closely related to these objectives.

The objective of self-realization.

The adolescent is striving to understand himself, to discover his abilities, aptitudes, potentialities, and to develop and utilize them.

The objective of human relationship.

The adolescent is also striving to be "popular with his peers," to find his proper place in his home, to prepare for future family responsibilities and to learn to enjoy a "rich, full and varied" social life.

The objective of economic efficiency.

This problem becomes increasingly acute for the adolescent, as improvement in technological methods postpones his entry into productive work. The

---

[7]Arthur I. Gates, et al., *Educational Psychology.* (New York: The Macmillan Company, 1942), p. 629.

adolescent boy is endeavoring to determine the type of work for which he is best fitted; how he can secure needed occupational information; how he can obtain required training; how he can acquire appropriate work experience; how he can secure a job and succeed in it.

The objective of civic responsibility.

The adolescent realizes the importance of membership on a team, in a grade, in a class and in extracurricular youth organizations. He anticipates the need to be a member of civic, church and other community groups. He is learning also the importance of participating in student body, city, state and national government; and is becoming increasingly aware of the importance of being a cooperative member of the world community.

A guidance program, devoted to the achievement of these four basic objectives of education, will help adolescent boys and girls to satisfy their needs as maturing individuals. The guidance program of the modern secondary school attempts to accomplish these goals.

SECTION D. ESSENTIAL CHARACTERISTICS OF A GUIDANCE PROGRAM.

A carefully worked out guidance program in the secondary school will have many of the following characteristics:

Definite Purposes.

1. The guidance program will facilitate the achievement of the basic objectives of education in a democratic society.
2. The guidance program will recognize youth characteristics and provide for the needs of boys and girls.

3. Teachers, counselors, administrators and others responsible for guidance will look upon all guidance activities, such as tests, records, ratings, marks, group guidance and counseling, not as ultimates, but as means for adjusting the school program to the needs of the students.

Appropriate Organization.

1. The organization for guidance in a particular school or district will be developed with primary consideration for the purposes to be served.
2. The particular type of program developed will reflect that unique combination of school and community resources which best serves the above purposes.
3. The guidance organization will depend upon:
   a. Size of the school.
   b. Training of the staff.
   c. Interest of the staff in guidance activities.
   d. Philosophy of the school district with respect to guidance.
   e. Opportunities for in-service education of those responsible for guidance.

Three basic types of organization are commonly accepted. Examples of these are illustrated in Appendix A.

Appropriate Administrative Arrangements.

1. Responsibility for guidance activities in a larger district should be delegated to a member of the school staff.
2. Final responsibility must be accepted by the chief administrator of the district for the organization and administration of guidance activities.
3. Those who participate in the guidance program will be represented in the planning, especially for those activities in which they participate most directly.

4. The guidance program will be continuous and consistent in all grades.

5. Definite provisions for guidance will be made in the master program, since guidance cannot become an actuality unless arrangement be made in "time and space," for example:

Teacher	Subject	Periods	Room
Miss Brown	Counseling	3 and 4	104

Systematic Techniques for Gathering Guidance Information.

1. Information about all students will be gathered in a planned, systematic way.

2. Plans will be made to collect data regarding all phases of student experiences such as: physical, academic, emotional, social, family and vocational, and home background.

3. Appropriate use will be made of methods of gathering guidance information such as:

   a. A testing program.
   b. Cumulative records.
   c. The interview.
   d. Observation and recording of student behavior.
   e. Autobiography.
   f. Questionnaire.
   g. The case study

Suggested Techniques for Administrative Use of Guidance Data.

Systematic methods of using guidance data will be developed and employed. These will include:

1. Establishment of a definite promotional policy, which will advance students through the grades according

to their age and ability, with a minimum of retardation or acceleration.

2. Coordination of data-gathering devices with record forms, so that essential information about each student will be economically and systematically accumulated for the use of all teachers.

3. Summary and distribution of cumulative data so that they will be directly available to all administrators, teachers and counselors responsible for guidance.

4. Utilization of guidance data that will result in a continuing program of curriculum revision.

Appropriate Use of Group Techniques in the Guidance Program.

Plans will be made to make use of group guidance techniques where these will contribute to the effectiveness of the guidance program. Among these may be the home room, exploratory courses, the orientation classes, assembly programs and other techniques.

Systematic Techniques for Use of Guidance Data with Individuals.

Opportunities will be provided at appropriate intervals for each student to discuss, with a counselor or teacher, problems of physical health and mental health, educational guidance, vocational planning and other problems which are of paramount interest to the student.

The counseling process will be regarded as an interaction between student and counselor in which the student is assisted to make plans in the light of his aptitudes, capacities, interests, aspirations and opportunities.

In-Service Growth of Staff.

The guidance program will provide for the continuous in-service growth in guidance techniques for all members of the staff.

Interpretation to the Community.

1. The guidance program will be designed to enlist the cooperation of the home and of community agencies which serve youth.

2. Definite plans will be made for interpreting guidance information to the community and for securing guidance information from community agencies.

Evaluation of the Guidance Program.

1. Arrangements will be made to evaluate the effectiveness of the guidance program:

   a. In terms of the quantity and quality of guidance activities provided in the school.

   b. In terms of its contribution to the improvement of student adjustment and behavior.

Suggested References.

California State Reconstruction and Reemployment Commission, *Postwar Objectives of Public Education in California.* Unpublished report, The Commission, Sacramento 14, February, 1945.

Commission on Teacher Education, *Physiological Aspects of Child Growth and Development.* Division on Child Development and Teacher Personnel; Washington, D. C.: American Council on Education, June, 1941, (mimeographed).

Educational Policies Commission, *The Purposes of Education in American Democracy.* Washington, D. C.: National Education Association, 1938.

Gates, Arthur I., et al, *Educational Psychology.* New York: The Macmillan Company, 1942.

Traxler, Arthur E., *Techniques of Guidance.* New York: Harper and Brothers, 1945.

CHAPTER II

TECHNIQUES FOR COLLECTING AND RECORDING GUIDANCE DATA

In this chapter seven techniques for collecting and recording guidance data are presented in the following sections:

The Testing Program.

The Interview.

Observation and Recording of Student Behavior.

Autobiography.

Questionnaire.

The Case Study.

Cumulative Records.

It should be stressed that still other techniques for collecting information, not discussed here, may be used as needed by the teacher and counselor. Among these are the following:

1. Teacher constructed objective and essay tests.
2. Student themes and reports.
3. Records of books read.
4. Summaries of leisure-time activities.
5. Samples of poems, drawings.
6. Check lists and rating scales.
7. Anecdotal records.
8. Attitude scales.
9. Records of work experience.

The administrator and his staff have the responsibility of determining which of the above techniques will be most effective in his school situation.

SECTION A. THE TESTING PROGRAM.

A Testing Program Defined.

A testing program is a systematic plan for administering, scoring and interpreting measures of mental maturity, skills, achievement, knowledges, interests, personal-social adjustment and special aptitudes. Such a program, carried on from year to year, makes it possible to measure more adequately the attainment of some of the goals of education.

A Testing Program Serves Student, Teacher, Administrator and Parent.

1. The student is helped to arrive, in an objective manner, at a better understanding of his capabilities, limitations and progress.

2. The teacher is helped to understand the capabilities and needs of the individual student and to make more effective judgments about his work. In addition, the teacher is guided in selecting appropriate materials and procedures for each class and class member.

3. The administrator is provided with information concerning educational strengths and weaknesses of a class, a grade, a school, or the school district as a whole. Upon occasion the administrator may find such information useful in a professional interpretation of the school program to the community.

4. The counselor is provided with basic information without which any guidance program is inadequate.

5. The program provides information which should be used in interpreting the needs of the individual student to his parents. It is obvious, however, that the teacher or administrator supplying the information must use judgment and discretion as to the type and amount of information to release.

What Do Tests Measure?

1. **Mental maturity.** Tests of mental maturity measure scholastic or learning ability.

2. **Achievement.**

   a. Tests of achievement in skills measure accomplishment in the basic educational tools: reading, arithmetic and language. Other skills less easily measured are those such as critical thinking, work-study habits and the like.

   b. Tests of information measure fields of knowledge, such as science or health. Such measurement of achievement has significance both for educational and vocational purposes.

3. **Interest.** Inventories of preferred activities aid the student in achieving desirable and significant objectives. Such inventories stimulate the development of interest and give direction to counseling as well as to the guidance program.

4. **Personality and mental health.** These inventories help to indicate the more intangible characteristics of the individual such as personal and social adjustment.

5. **Aptitude.** Tests of aptitude estimate potential ability in art, music, mechanical dexterity and in other capacities.

Suggested Testing Programs.

1. A satisfactory **minimum** testing program consists of the following:

   a. An intelligence or mental maturity test administered every three or four years.

   b. A diagnostic achievement test (providing information about reading, mathematics and language) administered every other year.

2. A satisfactory **comprehensive** testing program consists of the following:

   a. An intelligence or mental maturity test administered every two or three years.

   b. A diagnostic achievement test (providing data on reading, mathematics and language) administered every year or every other year.

   c. An interest inventory administered at least every three years.

   d. An inventory of social-personal adjustment administered every two or three years.

   e. Such special aptitude tests as may be indicated for a particular student.

Procedures for Carrying on An Effective Testing Program.

1. Selecting the Tests.

   a. A test is a set of prescribed tasks designed specifically to measure certain qualities, capacities, learnings or skills of an individual student or group of students.

   A standardized test is one for which the means of giving and scoring are rigidly prescribed and for which representative norms of known accuracy and reliability have been secured. Such a test may or may not be composed of an adequate sampling of tasks for any one particular individual. Therefore, if adequate measures of the abilities of individuals are to be obtained, it is necessary that students be retested from time to time with other test forms or different tests.

   b. There are many standardized tests which can be used in a testing program. It is important, therefore, that the selection of tests be on the basis of the following criteria:

      (1) The area of growth in which measures are needed.

      (2) The characteristics of the group to be tested, such as language handicaps, social background and the like.

      (3) The ease of administering and scoring.

      (4) The costs of tests and testing.

      (5) The validity and reliability of tests. (See the Appendix for a list of recommended tests.)

      (6) The ease of interpretation: availability of adequate norms and the like.

2. Administering the Testing Program.

    a. Personnel responsible for testing.

      (1) Responsibility for the administration of tests usually rests with the classroom teacher. Teachers may meet in groups for training or may be given individual help. The Coordinator of Research and Guidance or a school administrator serves as an advisor in training.

      (2) Superintendents, principals and counselors assume different degrees of responsibility for the testing program, depending upon the size and organization of the district. The purchase of test materials, distribution of materials to teachers, collection of materials and scheduling of testing periods are among the functions of administrators and counselors.

      (3) The Coordinator of Research and Guidance will provide assistance upon request.

    b. Techniques for giving the tests.

      (1) The details of test administration are available in the manuals accompanying the tests. Such details should be checked with the list "Strength-

ening Objective Testing Procedures" in the Appendix. Instructions in the test manual should be followed carefully.

(2) When machine-scored tests are administered, the following items need attention:

(a) Special machine-scoring pencils must be used in marking the answer pages.

(b) A demonstration should be given to make sure that the students know how to use the separate answer page.

(c) Each answer must be indicated by a solid black mark between the small dotted lines rather than by crosses or checks.

c. The environment for testing.

(1) The testing environment should approach the normal classroom situation as closely as possible.

(a) Test results may be invalidated when tests are administered to large groups of students in an auditorium, gymnasium or cafeteria.

(b) Careful attention should be given to seating facilities, ventilation, acoustics, lighting and heating.

(c) The approach made by the teacher to the testing situation should be calm, friendly and encouraging.

d. Best time to administer tests.

(1) Information secured from tests is most useful early in the school year when it may be used for:

(a) Diagnosing individual and group needs.

(b) Selecting teaching materials.

(c) Determining instructional procedures.

(2) Tests may be given at other times when further information is needed. (When test materials are to be processed through the County Office, certain schedules must be made for times other than early in the school year. The Coordinator of Research and Guidance will assist in the planning required for County service.)

(3) A year-to-year program of systematic measurement provides a continuous record of student growth.

3. Scoring the Tests. (The suggestions listed below apply especially to materials sent to the County Office for processing but equally well in other instances.)

    a. Hand-scoring.

       (1) Adherence to the specific directions for hand-scoring given in the test manual is of the utmost importance.

       (2) A careful check is necessary to insure the use of the proper scoring keys when more than one form of a test is being scored.

       (3) It is advisable to score all tests section by section rather than to score a complete test at one time.

       (4) Whenever feasible, a second person should re-score all or a part of the tests to eliminate errors in the scoring.

       (5) Clerical suggestions:

          (a) When raw scores are changed to percentile or grade placement scores, the operation should be checked frequently.

          (b) When data are recorded from test booklets, it is imperative that the **correct** data be recorded—that is, that raw scores should be recorded as **raw scores** rather than **I.Q.'s,** and the like.

(6) When the results of hand-scored tests are to be sent to the County Office for further analysis, the following procedure should be used:

(a) **Hand-scored** Intelligence Tests:
Test results should be reported in terms of I. Q.'s, mental ages and mental age grade placements for the language section, non-language section and total test, whenever possible. These data should be recorded alphabetically for the students of a class **on a special form provided by the County Office.**

If it is not feasible for the teacher to calculate mental ages or I. Q.'s, the front pages (or the pages listing the section scores and the total scores) should be torn from the test booklets and arranged alphabetically for the students of a class. It is not necessary to send in the complete booklet.

It is imperative that the age in months (or years and months) at the time of testing be provided for each student.

(b) **Hand-scored** Achievement Tests:
Test results should be reported in terms of grade placement scores rather than raw scores when possible. The data should be listed alphabetically for a class **on a special form provided by the County Office.**

(c) When intelligence tests have not been given **with** the achievement test, but when expectancy analyses are desired, the necessary intelligence data should be listed in the proper position on the special form.

I. Q.'s which are not too old will be brought up-to-date in terms of mental age, by the County Office.

The age of each student at testing time should be provided in months or in years and months.

(d) Other **hand-scored** tests:

Test results should be reported in terms of percentile scores, grade placement, standard scores, or other scores used in the interpretation of the particular test, rather than in raw scores. The data should be listed alphabetically for a class **on the form provided by the publisher of the test.**

(e) The analysis is facilitated when data are recorded as indicated above. If the data are provided in a form other than requested, or if the county forms are not used, much valuable time is lost in changing the scores and in recopying data on the correct forms, because such forms have been designed to conform to the tabulating machinery. The time for analysis is further reduced by listing students alphabetically and by supplying the correct ages and related information.

b. Preparation for machine-scoring.

Before submitting materials to the County Office for machine-scoring, the teacher or examiner should be responsible for the following:

(1) The original markings should be erased completely when changes in answers are made by the student.

(2) All random markings or scribbling on the answer pages should be erased.

(3)   Answer sheets should be arranged alphabetically, by students, and then grouped according to teacher and grade. The answer sheets should not be folded, creased, stapled or clipped. All materials should be packaged in durable containers for transit to the County Office.

(4)   Accurate chronological ages at the time of testing should be supplied in terms of months or years and months. Birthdates, when called for, should be given as month, day and year. All pertinent data, such as student names and the like, should be verified before forwarding to County Office.

(5)   Hand-scored sections of machine-scored tests should be **corrected accurately before** sending to County Office, with attention to the precautions listed under hand-scoring above.

(6)   The Test Data Verification Sheet, shown in the Appendix, should be filled in and forwarded with the test materials. Copies are available from the County Office or the Coordinator of Research and Guidance.

4. Summarizing the Test Results.

a. Definitions of terms used in connection with test summary sheets.

(1)   **Meaning of scores**—test scores are generally expressed first in terms of raw scores (scores obtained from a particular test). Raw scores, in and of themselves, are quite meaningless, because they cannot be compared directly with other test scores. A score of 140 on Test A, for example, cannot be interpreted unless some additional information is given. A score of 140 may be the lowest, the highest, or any score

between high and low for a particular group.
Raw scores are given meaning by changing
them into so-called **derived scores**—scores which
may be compared from test to test. Thus a raw
score may be changed into a rank within a
group by calling it the first or fifth in a group
of twenty-five. More frequently the percentile
rank is used—a rank which indicates roughly
the percentage of the group that falls below a
given score. Thus a percentile rank of 60 is
interpreted to mean that 60 per cent of the
group have earned lower scores. Knowledge
that a score on Test A is 140 is valueless. But
when the score of 140 is changed to a percentile
rank of 60 it takes on meaning. Other forms
of derived scores include age scores and grade
scores.

(2) **Chronological age (C.A.)** is the age in months
at which the student took a test. These ages
should be provided by the teacher when hand-
scored data are submitted for analysis. When
tests are machine-scored the ages will be calculated by the County Office—if the required information is placed on the answer sheet by the
student or teacher. When the teacher calcu-
lates the age he should keep in mind that the
months are added to the years on the basis
of the nearest 15 days. Thus if a student's
birthday (14 years) is on September 2 and he
takes a test on September 12, his chronological
age (C.A.) at test time is 14 years or 168 months.
However, if he takes the test on September 17,
his age is 14 years and 1 month or 169 months.
His test date is 15 days (or more) away from
his birthdate; therefore, another month is added

to his age. (Since chronological age is based on a twelve-month calendar year, use 14-1 to signify fourteen years and one month. Note that 14.1 is used to signify grade placement, i.e., the first month of the fourteenth grade and should not be used to express age.)

A more difficult case is the student whose birthday is April 29 (15 years) and who takes a test on the following November 7. The period of time from April 29 to October 29 is 6 months. The November 7 date is less than 15 days beyond October 29 so that no additional month is added. Therefore, the student's C.A. at test time is 15 years and 6 months or 186 months. If he had taken the test on November 20, his C.A. would have become 15 years and 7 months or 187 months (since November 20 is 15 or more days beyond October 29). The calculation of C.A. is facilitated by tables designed for this purpose. These tables may be secured from the Coordinator of Research and Guidance on request.

(3) **Mental age (M.A.)** is the age equivalent of an intelligence test raw score. The typical student of a given chronological age will make a certain number of correct responses to the items of a test. Mary's C.A. is 14 years and 10 months or 178 months. If she makes as many correct responses on an intelligence test as the average pupil of 15 years and 8 months, she is awarded a mental age of 15 years and 8 months or 188 months. Thus Mary's mental age depends upon how she scores in relation to the individuals upon whom the test was standardized.

(4) **Intelligence quotient (I.Q.)** is a measure of the mental brightness of an individual, i.e., a measure of the relationship of mental age to chronological age. It is found by dividing mental age by chronological age and multiplying by 100. Thus if Henry has a mental age of 15 years and 8 months or 188 months when he is actually 15 years and 8 months or 188 months of age at the time of testing, his I.Q. is 100 —188 M.A. divided by 188 C.A. multiplied by 100. (It is to be noted that the highest C.A. used in calculating I.Q. is that for 16 years, or 192 months. This adjustment is made necessary by the fact that average mental age tapers off at about 16 years of age. Use of C.A.'s higher than 192 months would, therefore, tend to reduce the I.Q.'s when such reduction is not warranted).

Average I.Q.'s tend to center about 100 and characterize the average learner. Higher I.Q.'s characterize individuals who are older mentally than they are chronologically and who are inclined to be rapid or very rapid learners. Lower I.Q.'s characterize individuals who are younger mentally than they are chronologically and who tend to be slow or very slow learners.

(5) **Grade placement (G.P.)** is the grade equivalent of a C.A., an M.A., or a test raw score. The typical student in a given school grade will make a certain number of correct responses to the items of a test. If Mary is in the third month of the ninth grade, her actual grade placement is 9.3. However, if she makes as many correct responses in arithmetic reasoning as the average student in the seventh month of the

tenth grade, her relative standing in arithmetic reasoning is a grade placement of 10.7. (Computed on the basis of a ten-month school year.) Actual grade placement refers to the specific month in the grade at the time the student took the test.

(6) **The average (Ave.)** is a single number, representing a whole group of scores, found by adding all the scores and dividing the total by the number of individuals who have received the scores. The average is also known as the "mean."

(7) **Deviation** is a number which represents the difference (how far above or below) between the score of an individual and some other figure such as the average for a group. Commonly, it is the difference between the grade placement obtained by a student on a test and his actual grade placement. His test grade placement may also be compared with the average placement of the class or any score expressed in grade placement. Thus, if Mary obtains a grade placement in reading comprehension of 10.7 when her actual grade placement is 10.2, she has a deviation of 10.7—10.2 or .5 (5 months) above her actual grade placement.

(8) **Expectancy**—averages and deviations from averages have limitations which affect their usefulness when small classes are involved. These limitations may be overcome by using deviations from expectancy for individuals or groups.

Expectancy involves the comparison of a student's actual measured achievement with his measured ability to achieve (both expressed in grade placements). Deviations from expectancy assume positive or negative values depending upon whether actual achievement is above or below the ability to achieve. (Such deviations are based on a ten-month school year.) This may be illustrated by examining the record of John, a ninth-grade student. If John's total reading achievement is equivalent to a grade placement of the eighth month of the ninth grade, while his mental age grade placement (ability to achieve) is equivalent to the eighth month of the eighth grade, John is achieving approximately one school grade above expectancy. (9.8—8.8 or 1.0 school grade, i.e., 10 months.) His deviation from expectancy, therefore, is +1.0. However, if John's total arithmetic achievement is equivalent to a grade placement of the ninth month of the seventh grade, while his mental age grade placement remains at the eighth month of the eighth grade, John is achieving approximately nine months below expectancy. (8.8—7.9 or .9 school grade, i.e., nine months.) His deviation from expectancy, therefore, is —.9. Errors of measurement occur when tests are given; therefore, too great a deviation from expectancy (or from teacher judgment) should be carefully examined to determine possible sources of error.

Because of the limitations of intelligence test results for students older than sixteen years of age, the expectancy concept should not be used above the ninth grade. There are other means available for determining whether students above the ninth grade are working up to capacity.

b. Forms for summarizing data:

(1) **Class Record Sheet**—this form provides space to list the chronological ages, chronological age grade placements, mental ages and mental age grade placements for a class of students. In addition, the grade placement scores for reading vocabulary, reading comprehension, total reading, arithmetic reasoning, arithmetic fundamentals, total arithmetic, language, spelling and total test may be recorded. Each of the spaces for the total reading, arithmetic, language and spelling scores is accompanied by a space in which the deviation from expectancy may be listed. Class averages are also provided on the form.

The form may be used to summarize data for teachers, grades, schools and districts as well as individual students in the classroom. A sample form has been placed in the Appendix.

(2) **Summary of Intelligence and Achievement**—this form provides space to tally I.Q. scores (both language and non-language), so the teacher may see the range of I.Q. and the average I.Q. for the classroom. Space is also provided for showing the range of chronological age, mental age and subject-matter achievements in terms of grade placement. Averages are obtained for each distribution. Deviations of the achievement averages from actual grade placement (the grade and month in which the student is enrolled) are calculated.

The form may be used to summarize data by grades, schools and district, as well as for a classroom. A sample form has been placed in the Appendix.

(3) **Analysis of Achievement in Relation to Expectancy**—this form indicates the number and per cent of students working at, above, or below expectancy. The student is placed in one of five expectancy deviation areas for each of four subject-matter achievements. Area 0 includes expectancy deviations from .5 (5 months) above expectancy to .5 (5 months) below expectancy. This area is regarded as indicating that achievement closely parallels expectancy. Thus if Mary obtains an expectancy deviation of —.4 in her total reading grade placement, she is classified in Area 0. The other expectancy areas are explained on the form which has been placed in the Appendix.

This form may be used to summarize data for teachers, grades and district, as well as for a classroom.

(4) **Age-Grade Analysis Form** provides space for tabulating individual students in terms of certain I.Q. levels and chronological age levels with respect to proper grade placement. The form is based on data about intelligence, age and grade placement accumulated in the County Office over a period of years. Completion of the form indicates whether a student is normally placed in his grade or is underage or overage.

The form may be used to summarize totals for grades, schools and district, as well as for the classroom. A sample form has been placed in the Appendix.

(5) Miscellaneous forms useful in summarizing test results are graphic grade placement charts and

special charts or graphs for reporting specific studies.

5. Using the Test Results.

a. Students are helped, through the proper interpretation of test results, to arrive objectively at a better understanding of their capacities and limitations.

b. The teacher uses tests results in:

(1) Understanding the range of abilities and achievements in his classroom.

(2) Selecting materials of appropriate difficulty for the range of abilities and achievements.

(3) Organizing groups for classroom activities.

(4) Locating certain difficulties which indicate the need for drill and added emphasis.

(5) Identifying students for special study, such as the student working seriously below expectancy or the student who is a reading problem.

c. The administrator uses test results in:

(1) Knowing the variations within his school.

(2) Obtaining suggestions for meeting the curricular needs of classes and schools.

(3) Securing data which are helpful in the organization of groups.

(4) Understanding the instructional problems of teachers.

(5) Providing a record of the continuity of educational growth and defining the needs of those students entering junior or senior high school.

(6) Interpreting the school program to the community upon occasion.

d. The counselor uses tests to help students plan more effectively in:

    (1) Securing impersonal judgments of student capacities and behavior.

    (2) Providing balanced data for use in conjunction with personal judgments and valuations.

e. Cautions for teachers and administrators in the use of test results:

    (1) Errors of measurement may invalidate a test score:

        (a) Any single score may be misleading.

        (b) A student should be retested when doubt arises as to the interpretation.

        (c) A test score should not be considered as a specific point since it actually may be a few points higher or lower than indicated.

        (d) Scores that differ from one application of a particular test to another may be obtained because the group being tested is not similar to the group on which the test was standardized or because there are differences in the way the test was administered.

        (e) Scores obtained from different tests may seldom be compared directly; measurements of growth for individuals should be secured from the same test.

    (2) Tests are not the only means of getting significant data about students.

    (3) It is usually more valuable to compare a particular student's attainment with his own ability to attain, or with his previous record, than to compare one student with another student.

    (4) The scores of some inventories, personality and others, should be interpreted cautiously, since such scores may not be as valid as those secured from other tests.

    (5) All test data should be treated professionally, or as confidential information. Good judgment, sincerity and tact should prevail in all interpretations of test data.

6. Services Available From the Division of Research and Guidance of the County Office upon the request of the district:

a. Consultant service:

    (1) Survey the district needs relative to a testing program.

    (2) Plan with district personnel in the organization of the testing program.

    (3) Assist with in-service teacher-training procedures for giving and scoring the tests and recording the data for purposes of interpretation.

    (4) Help in planning and making special studies.

b. Statistical service:

    (1) Scoring of tests of intelligence and achievement by machine—**all sections of tests which can be hand-scored should be completed by the district before sending the tests to the County Office.**

    (2) Computing the equivalents of intelligence and achievement test scores—this includes finding mental ages, intelligence quotients, mental age grade placements and other grade placements. Such data are recorded on the Class Record Sheet.

    (3) Combining intelligence and achievement data for survey purposes—this includes computation of expectancy deviations for individual students and recording of the data on the Class Record Sheet.

       (4) Summarizing the results of a testing program to indicate school and district achievement in relation to grade norms and expectancy.

  c. Interpretative service:

       (1) Analysis of abilities in relation to achievement.

       (2) Interpretation of analysis in cooperation with the teacher and administrator.

       (3) Interpretation of special studies.

Suggested References

Buros, Oscar, *The 1940 Mental Measurements Yearbook.* Highland Park, New Jersey: The Mental Measurements Yearbook, 1941.

Darley, John, *Testing and Counseling in the High School Guidance Program.* Chicago: Science Research Associates, 1943.

Lee, J. Murray, *A Guide to Measurement in Secondary Schools.* New York: D. Appelton-Century Company, 1936.

McCall, William, *Measurement.* New York: The Macmillan Company, 1938.

Remmers, H. H., and Gage, N. L., *Educational Measurement and Evaluation.* New York: Harper and Brothers, 1943.

Smith, E. R., and Tyler, R. W., *Appraising and Recording Student Progress.* New York: Harper and Brothers, 1943.

SECTION B.   THE INTERVIEW.

The Interview as a Technique for Collecting Information.

The interview is a purposeful conversation, a technique by which one individual may seek information from another. It may also be used to release tensions and change attitudes. (See the Counseling Process, Chapter V, Section C.) For purposes of this section, however, the interview will be considered as a technique for collecting guidance data.

The interview may be used effectively by any member of the school staff. Not all conversations, however, that take place in student-teacher relationships can be called interviews; many times the value of the interview goes unnoticed because it was not scheduled and held in a formal manner. The use of the interview is not limited to any group of people or condition of circumstances. With certain fundamental knowledges, this technique can be used effectively to collect pertinent guidance information.

Phases of Interviewing.

1. Preparation.
   a. It is as necessary to prepare for an interview as it is to prepare for teaching a lesson. This preparation should include the acquiring of a background of information about the student.
   b. The physical arrangements for the interview should produce an atmosphere of comfort and security. This would require elimination of outside disturbances, such as excessive noise or distracting influences. Privacy is essential in establishing a feeling of security and willingness to discuss freely the problems that have occasioned the interview. Comfortable chairs facing two sides of a table or desk usually constitute the most effective arrangement of furniture.

2. Initiating the Interview.
   a. The interview must begin with the establishment of a friendly relationship between counselor and counselee. In technical language this is known as establishing "rapport." It means that the burden is on the counselor to do and say the things necessary to accomplish this relationship. No pattern or plan can be set to do this effectively, since each counsel-

ing situation is different. Topics that have been effectively used to give the student initial confidence in starting the conversation are those with which he is entirely familiar, such as:

(1) School activity.

(2) Hobbies.

(3) Home town or state.

(4) Brothers and sisters.

(5) Significant achievements.

(6) Important current community activity.

(7) Work experience.

b. During the first few seconds of the interview, it is necessary for the counselor to make a decision as to what approach he should use in order to arrive at a successful conclusion. It can be said that during this period of "mental shadow-boxing," the strategy of the interview must be planned.

3. Conducting the Interview.

Although a specific pattern or plan cannot be established, a counselor will find the following suggestions helpful:

a. Discuss willingly the stated problem of student but watch for unstated or implied problems.

b. Help the student to identify his problem.

c. Remember that the student did not come to listen. Do not monopolize the conversation.

d. Use impersonal rather than personal references wherever possible.

e. Note that the interview is not a cross-examination of the student.

f. Keep vocabulary of the interview on the student's level.

g. Retain control of the interview without dominating it.

h. Appraise student reactions such as facial expression, eyes, voice and posture.

i. Watch for what is avoided or **not** said as well as what **is** said.

j. Answer factual questions with factual information.

k. Admit it if you do not know, but be willing to help find the answer.

l. Give unfavorable facts when necessary, but stress ability and minimize disability.

m. Avoid generalities, be specific.

n. Assist the student to lay out alternate plans so that there will be an opportunity for him to make a decision.

o. Help the student to pick out significant facts, developed during the interview.

p. Summarize or have the student summarize the interview as a means for determining a plan of action.

4. Closing the Interview.

This phase of the interview is important because it may affect the attitude of the student.

a. It will be impossible to solve all the student's problems at any one interview. It is better to help him with one problem at a time.

b. When the student leaves the interview, he should feel that he would like to return with other problems.

5. Recording the Interview.

The record of the interview should be as simple as possible and yet take in all the basic items that will be useful in the future, such as:

a. Date of the interview (10-15-47).

b. The incident or problem that brought about the initial interview.

c. Pertinent reactions observed by the counselor.

d. What was accomplished during the interview.

e. Plans of action to be taken to serve as a basis for future interviews with the student.

f. Signature of person recording data.

Summary.

The interview is a purposeful conversation, a technique by which one individual may seek information from another. It can be used by any member of the staff as a means of getting and giving information. To carry through an interview effectively, attention should be given to: (1) careful preparation, (2) establishment of a friendly relationship, (3) use of appropriate interviewing procedures, (4) suitable method of terminating the interview, and (5) provision for recording the highlights of the interview.

Suggested References.

Bingham, Walter V., and Moore, Bruce V., *How to Interview*. New York: Harper and Brothers, 1941.

Darley, John G., *Testing and Counseling in the High School Guidance Program*. Science Research Associates, Chicago, 1943.

Lefever, D. Welty, et al., *Principles and Techniques of Guidance*. New York: Ronald Press Company, 1941.

Myers, George E., *Principles and Techniques of Vocational Guidance*. New York: McGraw-Hill Book Company, 1941.

Rogers, Carl R., *Counseling and Psychotherapy*. Boston: Houghton-Mifflin Company, 1942.

Traxler, Arthur E., *Techniques of Guidance*. New York: Harper and Brothers, 1945. Pp. 25-28.

Williamson, E. G., *How to Counsel Students*. New York: McGraw-Hill Book Company, 1939.

SECTION C.   OBSERVATION AND RECORDING OF STUDENT BEHAVIOR.

Observation as a Technique for Collecting Guidance Data.

Teachers, supervisors and educators in general are being encouraged to give more attention to the observation of students in learning situations. The guidance worker, also, needs to make more extensive use of this technique.

Observation is the process of coming to know the student and his problems by studying his behavior in particular situations. The process involves the following:

1. Having a purpose for observation.
2. Preparing for the observation.
3. Watching for significant behavior.
4. Analyzing and summarizing the observed behavior.
5. Making a satisfactory record.

Making Significant Observations.

1. All behavior is a reaction or response to stimulation. From the point of view of the qualified observer, behavior is a symptom—a guidepost to some related factor or cause. One of the principal problems of the teacher, as an observer and as a guide or director of the learning process, is learning how to distinguish the real causes of behavior from the pseudo-causes or symptoms.

2. It is not possible to list in detail the types of behavior to be observed by a teacher or counselor. However, the following items should be helpful in indicating what is important to observe:

    a. Physical symptoms, such as defective vision.
       (1) Does he squint?

    (2) Does he hold book close to eyes?
    (3) Does he lack persistence in study?

b. Symptoms of educational adjustment.
    (1) Does he show ability to learn work of the grade?
    (2) Is he able to follow directions?
    (3) Does he understand assignments?

c. Symptoms of social and emotional adjustment.
    (1) How does the student get along with others?
    (2) What is his initiative?
    (3) How does he respond to directions?
    (4) Does he seem secure in his relationships?
    (5) Is he self-reliant?

d. In general, records of behavior are valuable in relation to health, interests, achievement and social activities.

Improving Observational Techniques.

1. Strive for objectivity in observation.

    a. Development of an awareness of the subjective nature of personal observation made by teachers and counselors.

        (1) The teacher or counselor interprets stimuli as understanding or perceptions. The quality of his perceptions and of his interpretations is related to his background of experience, values, attitudes and maturity. As a result, he may, unknowingly, be reading his personal ideas into the conduct of his students. For example, a teacher may interpret the enthusiastic behavior of a student of Spanish-American descent as an attempt to mask qualities of shiftlessness which he (the teacher) believes to be characteristic of all such people. Name-calling and

labeling of behavior as "lazy," "stubborn" and the like are to be avoided.

(2) The observer should endeavor to define his concepts, and recognize and clarify his own assumptions about behavior. Behavior of different types carries social and moral implications which are often unwarranted from a scientific point of view. The competent observer must study behavior scientifically. This requires training and a thorough examination of personal biases, "pet peeves" and preconceived notions. Through this procedure proper perspective will be acquired and insight into the real meanings of behavior will be enhanced.

(3) The trained observer does not hesitate to use and to develop devices or instruments which rectify his limitations in recall, association, logical reasoning and reaction time.

b. A higher degree of objectivity may be attained by:
   (1) Definition and clarification of the concepts used.
   (2) Awareness of the purposes of the particular observation.
   (3) Practice and guidance in making observations.
   (4) Use of analyses and descriptions.
   (5) Adoption of instruments or devices for testing and evaluation.
   (6) Application of graphical and statistical methods in determining trends and relationships.

2. Utilize techniques for describing and recording behavior.
   a. Devices for making controlled observations may vary from simple questions, which give direction to the observation of students in particular situations, to

more complicated tests and laboratory-type instruments.

b. Devices for recording descriptions and evidences.

   (1) The simplest device for teacher record consists of a small pad of paper. The teacher uses such a pad to record on-the-spot observations and files the slip in the student's folder.

   (2) Other devices include rating scales, check lists, analysis forms, interview record sheets, anecdotal records, cumulative records and the like.

   (3) A device which is extremely helpful in aiding the observer to maintain his observations separate from his interpretations is the anecdotal record:

Date	Situation	Description of behavior	Possible Explanation	Observer
10/2/46	Painting	H destroyed his painting when asked to show it to the class.	Does H fear criticism or feel he is inadequate?	J. W.

It is highly advisable to retain behavior descriptions separate from interpretations so that others may make their own interpretations.

c. Preservation of samples of student work.

Samples of work in art, written expression, free response to questions and the like become objects for interpretation as to probable meanings.

3. Utilize techniques for facilitating appraisal and judgment.

   a. Devices for improving judgments.

Scales, grade or age norms, percentile norms, standards and the like provide objective criteria for making judgments, in contrast to reliance on personal experiences and impressions.   See Section A of this chapter for elaboration.

b. Estimates of the reliability of judgments.
All observations have varying degrees of accuracy. Knowledge of accuracy in judgments may be obtained through the application of certain statistical formulas.

c. Long-term reporting of behavior.
In view of the continuous change and on-going nature of education, the competent observer will gather his data over a long period of time so that definite patterns and trends may emerge.

4. Be cautious in making observations.

a. The significance of observations depends upon the abilities, understandings and characteristics of the observer.

b. The observer needs to be conscious of the danger of misinterpretation through the confusion of symptoms with underlying causes.

c. Recordings of observations should be made promptly, so that none of the important details will be forgotten.

d. Generalizations from observation should be arrived at only after careful study.   Such generalizations should be held to a minimum.

e. Effective observation frequently requires that memory, reasoning and other intellectual factors of the observer be supplemented by devices in the form of check lists, tests, report forms and the like.

f. It is desirable to record behavior symptoms in descriptive and objective terms rather than in general terminology such as "troublesome," "mischievous" and the like.

g. Flexibility of techniques should be cultivated with a consequent reduction of dogmatic application.

5. While the teacher or counselor may not be able to make use of all the techniques outlined, he will proceed with a realization of their importance to good observation.

Summary.

Observation is the process of coming to know the student and his problems, in particular situations, through activities which involve purpose, awareness, understanding and proper recording. The qualified observer recognizes the personal nature of the process. He strives to acquire a more scientific attitude, and uses devices which help him to make his judgments more valid.

Suggested References.

Commission on Teacher Education, *Helping Teachers to Understand Children*. Division on Child Development and Teacher Personnel, Washington, D. C.: American Council on Education, 1945.

Los Angeles County Superintendent of Schools, "The Reading Process." Bulletin No. 8093; Los Angeles, 12: Division of Research and Guidance, May, 1940.

Traxler, Arthur E., *Techniques of Guidance*. New York: Harper and Brothers, 1945.

Woodworth, Robert S., *Psychology*. New York: Henry Holt & Company, 1940.

SECTION D. AUTOBIOGRAPHY.

Making Use of the Autobiography.

Counselors and other guidance personnel have occasionally found the autobiography a very effective device for securing pertinent information that might otherwise have been overlooked. This device offers the student an opportunity to express in his own words information not gained from tests or by other formal means. When carefully used, this technique can assist the counselor or teacher to gain a better understanding of the student's abilities, interests, ambitions and personal problems.

In addition to the personal information gained about a student, the autobiography lays a foundation for an effective interview between counselor and student. Since it is also a mental hygiene exercise in itself, the autobiography may enable the student to take a more objective view of himself and his problems.

The assignment of writing an autobiography may be given by the student's counselor, the home-room or guidance teacher, the English or Social Studies teacher, or even by some other teacher. It should not be attempted, however, by any teacher until the confidence, attentive interest and respect of the student have been gained. The teacher should, in every case, make it clear to each student that the autobiography is to be considered confidential guidance material and, as such, will be treated in a professional manner, and used only for the student's welfare and benefit. The student must be fully aware that in no case does a counselor or teacher have a desire to pry into his private life.

Methods for Securing the Autobiography.

The method used for securing the autobiography will of necessity vary on different school levels and in different schools. Whatever the form or method used, it should be attempted only after a period of preparation and develop-ment of student interest in and knowledge of the purposes and uses of the autobiography.

The best time for writing the autobiography should be early in the student's first semester in a new school. How-ever, sufficient time should have elapsed for him to have acquired a feeling of ease and security.

The autobiography may be a life narrative. The student will be assisted if the counselor or teacher making the as-signment will provide a brief outline, such as:

1. Early history of the student.
2. Family background and history.
3. Health and physical record.
4. School history.
5. Interests, leisure time activities, hobbies, travel expe-riences, friendships.
6. Occupational experiences.
7. Educational plans for the future.
8. Long-time vocational plans.
9. Desires and plans regarding marriage and home life.

Applying the Autobiography in Guidance Situations.

The counselor or guidance teacher will, of course, have access to the autobiography, which has been filed in the student's cumulative record folder. The counselor can study and analyze the autobiography. From it can be determined the student's ability to recognize assets and liabilities and to deal with personal problems. In addition the counselor may arrive at an understanding of the student's attitude toward home, school, community and life in general.

Analysis of the autobiography should disclose problems needing further study. It is significant to note omissions, as they are often indicative of difficulties.

Sometimes items are exaggerated out of proportion to their real significance even though they may indicate imaginary difficulties and needs. They need attention, however, because, to that particular student, they are real and require adjustive guidance.

Student responses in the autobiography may be verified in some cases by making a home visit and including in the interview casual questions regarding certain doubtful items in the autobiography. Counselors or teachers may also secure correct information regarding these items by means of conferences with the student.

Summary.

The autobiography furnishes student information not obtainable by group or individual test means. It provides an understanding of the student's interests, abilities, personal history, hopes, ambitions and desires, and may disclose personal problems requiring guidance. It is a technique which serves as a mental health exercise by stimulating the student to adopt an objective view of himself and his environment.

Suggested References.

Hamrin, Shirley, and Erickson, Clarence E., *Guidance in the Secondary School*, New York: D. Appleton-Century Company, 1939. Pp. 95-96.

Schmaelzle, O. I., Editor, *A Guide to Counseling*, San Francisco: San Francisco Public Schools, 1944. Pp. 53-54.

SECTION E.   THE QUESTIONNAIRE IN GUIDANCE.

Values. The questionnaire facilitates the work of the counselor and other guidance persons by:

1. Providing a controlled interview technique which discloses much necessary information.

2. Shortening the time necessary in interviewing each student individually.

3. Bringing to light the answers to questions of a personal and social nature regarding students that otherwise would require much questioning.

Suggestions for Use.

1. In order to be an **effective** instrument, the questionnaire:
   a. Should ask for available information.
   b. Should be meaningful to the student.
   c. Should elicit answers that are short, specific and definite.
   d. Should request impersonal and factual information.

2. The guidance department of each high school should formulate the questionnaire to:
   a. Suit its own specific purposes.
   b. Gather usable data.
   c. Make critical information readily available.
   d. Follow the sequence of the cumulative record folder so as to facilitate recording.

In the high schools the students must generally be depended upon to fill out the questionnaire. Adequate supervision, however, is imperative.

Purposes and Uses.

It is quite important that the purposes and uses of the questionnaire be explained to the students in order to secure their cooperation and understanding. They should know that the requested information is for their guidance and assistance by the counselors, and that these data will be treated in a thoroughly professional and confidential manner by the counselors. For this reason, then, it is wise to have a preparation or orientation period preceding the time of the actual filling in of the questionnaire form.

Summary.

The strategic time for administering the **general information** questionnaire should be early during the first semester of a student's stay in the school, but late enough for him to have become acquainted with his teachers and school situation and to have developed a sense of security and confidence. Questionnaires on special problems, such as those dealing with vocational interests and work experience, may be utilized when the need has arisen.

Frequently the questionnaire data may have to be supplemented or revised by the parents. Accuracy of replies is to be desired. Sometimes it is possible to correct minor errors of record by tactful telephone conversations. Many times it is wise to have the questionnaire corrected or brought up-to-date, especially after a year or two has elapsed. All changes or new information should be dated. This, then, should be followed through by correcting or bringing up-to-date the cumulative record.

Suggested References.

Lefever, D. Welty, et al., *Principles and Techniques of Guidance*. New York: The Ronald Press Company, 1941. P. 499.

Traxler, A. E., *Techniques of Guidance*. New York: Harper and Brothers, 1945. Pp. 28-41.

Williamson, E. G., *How to Counsel Students*. New York: McGraw-Hill Book Company, 1939. Pp. 318-19, 355, 413, 433, 468-69.

A Suggested Personal Questionnaire for Secondary School Use follows:

A SUGGESTED PERSONAL QUESTIONNAIRE FOR SECONDARY SCHOOL USE

Student's name...Date....................
Address.. Class..............
Date of birth..Place of birth................
School District..................... School...........Sex...........Age...........

A. Home and Family.

1. Father's name............................Address............................
   Occupation (write "deceased" if not living)....................
2. Mother's name............................Address............................
   Occupation (write "deceased" if not living)....................
3. With whom do you live? Please check: Father ( )
   Mother ( ) Stepmother ( ) Stepfather ( ) Aunt ( )
   Uncle ( ) Guardian ( ) Brother ( ) Sister ( ) Other....
4. How many brothers and sisters do you have? Number of brothers........Number of sisters........Number of brothers at home..............Number older..............Number younger............Number of sisters at home............Number older................Number younger................Number of brothers not living................Number of sisters not living..................
5. Name other people living in your home in addition to your immediate family (Roomer, friend or relative)
   ----
6. Circle, below, the highest grade your parents completed in school, for example: 6 7 (8) 9
   Father 0 1 2 3 4 5 6 7 8 9 10 11 12 13 14 15 16 16+
   Mother 0 1 2 3 4 5 6 7 8 9 10 11 12 13 14 15 16 16+
7. Please list the magazines which your family has at home regularly.

   ----

8. Please list the newspapers which your family has at home regularly..

B. School Activities:

1. Name the schools which you have attended...............
   ....
   ....
   ....

   (Give city and state for each)

2. Which school subjects do you enjoy most?......................
   Why?..

3. Which subjects do you dislike most?..................................
   Why?..

4. In which of the following activities are you taking part? (Mark with "X")
   In which of the following activities would you like to take part? (Mark with "V")

   ......1. Glee Club   ......8. Hiking Club
   ......2. Drama Club   ......9. Public speaking
   ......3. Stamp Club   ......10. Hi-Y
   ......4. Photography Club   ......11. Others..............
   ......5. Writers Club   ......12.   "   ....
   ......6. School paper   ......13.   "   ....
   ......7. Athletics (which ones) ......14.   "   ....
   ....
   ....

5. Do you plan to go to a commercial school, trade school, junior college or to college?..................................
   Which school or college?..........................What course do you plan to take?..

C. Vocational Plans:

1. What kind of work would you like to do for a living?
   ....

2. How long have you been interested in that type of work? ....

3. What started your interest? ....

4. What abilities or qualifications do you think you possess for that work? (Please be specific) ....
....

5. What school marks do you need to prepare for that work? ....

D. Leisure Time:

1. How much of your spare time do you spend reading?
None..............Little...........Some...........Very much...........

2. How often do you attend the movies? ....

3. Name five movies that you have enjoyed particularly during the past year. ....
....
....

4. Name two of your favorite actors...............................
....

5. Name two of your favorite actresses..........................
....

6. How much time do you spend daily listening to the radio?........................Hours?

7. What are your favorite radio programs?...................
....

8. What pets do you own?..

9. How much time do you spend taking care of pets?
....

10. Have you ever had private lessons of any kind?
In what?........................For how long?...................

11. What recreation do you enjoy most during your summer vacation?..

12. What are your favorite sports and games?...............
....

13. List the chores or regular jobs you do around your

home. ....

....

....

....

14. What do you and your family do together? Check with whom you do the following activities.

	Mother	Father	Brother	Sister	Alone	Others
Attend movies						
Attend church						
Take week-end trips						
Attend ball games						
Attend concerts						
Other activities						
....						
....						
....						

15. What are the usual topics of conversation at home? ....

16. Have you a best friend or pal?............Who is it?.......
....

17. Do you prefer to be with (Please check "V") older people............, people of the same age............, younger people............, yourself............

18. Are your friends mostly boys or girls?.................
19. What do you especially enjoy doing with a group of your friends?.................
20. How do you spend your spare time when you are alone? ....
21. Do you attend Sunday School?.............In what church activities do you take part?.................
.... Which church?.................
22. What organizations or clubs do you attend?.................
....
23. Do you entertain your friends at your home?.............
If so, how often?.................

E. Spending Money:

1. Do you receive spending money?.................
Regular weekly allowance?.................
Regular monthly allowance?.................
Only as you earn it?.........Only as you request it?.........
2. If you earn money, **how** do you earn it?.................
....
3. How many hours per week do you work?.................
4. Do your parents direct the spending of your money?
....
5. Do you pay for any of the following out of your own money? School lunches?............. Clothes?.............
School supplies?............... Anything else?.................
....
6. What do you do with what is left, if any?.................
....

F. Remarks, Comments, Explanations:

....
....
....
....

SECTION F. THE CASE STUDY.

Definition of a Case Study.

A case study is a careful analysis, by school, medical, and psychological personnel, of an individual's assets and liabilities. Its purpose is to assist the individual in making a more satisfactory adjustment in school, home and community. Two steps are involved:

1. Diagnosis.
   The student is studied in relation to his total environment, in an effort to discover causes for his maladjustment.

2. Treatment.
   An attempt is made, through cooperative thinking and planning, to outline treatment appropriate to the student's needs.

Which Students Should Be Studied.

Although, ideally, all students should have records comparable to those of a case study, limitations of time and personnel make this impossible. Consequently, only those students whose behavior and problems cannot adequately be handled by the classroom teacher and counselor should be referred for case study.

The Case Study, A Cooperative Enterprise.

The home visit required for securing Special Study[1] data should be made by a school nurse, social case worker, counselor, psychologist or other professionally trained person.

---

[1]Copies of the *Outline for Special Study*, developed and used by the staff of the Division of Research and Guidance, Los Angeles County Schools, may be secured by addressing a letter to Division of Research and Guidance, Office of Los Angeles County Superintendent of Schools, 808 N. Spring St., Los Angeles 12, California.

Generally, the Psychologist or Coordinator of Research and Guidance is the person trained and equipped to organize, analyze and coordinate all these objective data, to add the interpretation of individual psychological test information and to preside at the case conference.

At the case conference the following persons should be present:

1. Principal, vice principal or dean.
2. Teachers of the student being studied.
3. Counselor or director of research.
4. School physician.
5. School nurse.
6. Social case worker or home teacher.
7. Attendance and welfare officer.
8. Probation officer.
9. Representatives of community character-building organizations for youth.

Procedures for Case Study.

When a student fails to adjust satisfactorily in school, arrangements for a case study should be made with the Coordinator of Research and Guidance. Copies of the **Outline for Special Study,** No. 15040, will be supplied so that all needed data can be collected and recorded.

The following information should be included on the form:

1. Identification data:
   a. Name.
   b. Address.
   c. School district and school.
   d. Grade.
   e. Nationality.
   f. Birthdate.

    g. Parents' names.

    h. Signature of person requesting study.

    i. Date.

2. Reasons for the special study, such as: description, history and nature of difficulty.

3. Specific techniques or procedures already used by school to help student adjust.

4. Health record and report of physical examination.
    a. Data on file in nurse's office such as height, weight and the like.
    b. Data secured by physician's special examination, including specific health problems.

5. Educational record and test data.
    a. Cumulative record and attendance data.
    b. School marks.
    c. Classroom and extracurricular participation.
    d. Test data.

6. The student's behavior as revealed through observation and personality tests.
    a. Physical strength.
    b. Work habits.
    c. Ability to get along with people.
    d. Usual disposition.
    e. Evidence of emotional tension or mannerism.
    f. Self-confidence.
    g. Interests and abilities.
    h. Methods of discipline and control.
    i. Attitude toward failure and success.
    j. Cause of student's problem.

7. Social or family background record.
    a. Persons in the home, relationships.
    b. Age and education of each.
    c. Occupation and recreation of each.
    d. Family irregularities.

     e. Student's privacy for sleep and study.

     f. Educational and cultural status of home.

     g. Membership in community groups.

     h. Home and school relations.

     i. Parental attitudes, responsibility and discipline.

     j. General home conditions.

8. Parents' observations.

     a. Health problems.

     b. Ability to get along with associates.

     c. Interests and hobbies.

     d. Form of discipline.

     e. Reaction to success and failure.

     f. Approval of friends.

     g. Attitude toward school.

     h. Home responsibilities.

     i. Parents' statement of problem.

9. Follow-up.

     a. Progress of student and status of problem.

     b. Transfer to another school or district.

Using this **Outline for Special Study,** the psychologist or co-ordinator, in a private interview with the student, administers an individual Binet intelligence test and a performance test. It is important for certain types of cases that a personality or mental health test also be given. If the school has not already done so recently, it is desirable, where the problem is an educational one, to administer an achievement test, especially in reading. The interview should attempt to disclose specific information which will help in diagnosis and treatment of social and personal problems.

When all these data are recorded and analyzed, the psychologist or coordinator attempts to look at the total picture, and make certain diagnoses and tentative suggestions for treatment, and prepares a report for consideration at the case conference.

Case studies may be relatively simple or they may become quite elaborate, but at any rate, the data should be recorded accurately, and as complete as needed. This procedure requires trained personnel, confidential treatment and a professional attitude on the part of all who are involved in collection and use of the data.

Too much cannot be learned about a student, his life and habits and complete environment. Such evidence should be carefully weighed and considered from every point of view in a case conference.

It is often wise to determine what member of the school staff has the closest rapport with and understanding of the student and to capitalize upon that person as the prime guidance worker for this student.

Much understanding, kindness, wise planning, encouragement and guidance are necessary on the part of all who participate in a case study. Each should contribute information on the problem, and jointly, attempt to determine its cause, plan techniques and make recommendations for the best possible solution.

Summary.

Case study techniques are used for serious individual student problems which persist beyond group diagnostic methods. The purpose is two-fold: diagnosis and treatment. The technique requires trained personnel with professional attitude, and involves the recording of specific and objective data on an **Outline for Special Study.** Significant data are secured from a physical examination record, school and group test data, and a home visit made by a professionally trained nurse, social worker, counselor or psychologist. Additional information regarding intelligence, achievement and adjustment should be secured by an individual psychological examination.

An important part of the case study is the case conference, which should include those persons most closely in contact with the student. Such a conference is generally under the leadership of the examining psychologist who analyzes, coordinates, and interprets the findings and develops into a formal plan the consensus regarding recommendations. Follow-up and checking on the progress and placement of the student are an important part of the entire technique.

Suggested References.

Crow, Lester D., and Crow, Alice, *Mental Hygiene in Schools and Home Life.* New York: McGraw-Hill Book Company, 1942. Pp. 270-272.

Dunsmoor, C. C., and Miller, L. M., *Guidance Methods for Teachers.* Scranton: International Book Company, 1942. Pp. 277-291.

Fenton, Norman, *Mental Hygiene in School Practice.* Palo Alto, California: Stanford University Press, 1944. Pp. 64-91.

Schmaelzle, O. I., Editor, *A Guide to Counseling.* San Francisco: San Francisco Public Schools, 1944.

Tiegs, Ernest W., and Katz, Barney, *Mental Hyiene in Education.* New York: The Ronald Press Company, 1941. Pp. 190-200.

Traxler, A. E., *Techniques of Guidance.* New York: Harper and Brothers, 1945. Pp. 284-307.

SECTION G. THE CUMULATIVE RECORD SYSTEM.

What is a Cumulative Record System?

A cumulative record system is a plan for recording, filing and using information essential to the guidance of students. The information usually included in a cumulative record consists of data related to:

1. Identification of the student.
2. Health and physical development.

3. Home and family background.
4. Curricular experiences.
5. Aptitude and achievement.
6. Personal and social adjustment.

Importance of Cumulative Records.

Cumulative records assure a long-term professional approach to guidance. They aid the teacher to become acquainted with his students. Such records facilitate discovery of students with special abilities or disabilities as well as direct provision for individual differences. Cumulative records offer a basis for confidential reports to outside specialists or clinics, assist the teacher to interpret student characteristics to parents, and make possible more complete records to other schools.

From an adequate cumulative record system, school personnel can present a complete record to the Court for the small percentage of students who will be subject to legal action. When a petition is filed against a minor, a report form is sent immediately to the school, asking that the Juvenile Court and Probation Department, and Juvenile Hall if the minor is detained, be given as complete a school record as is available. This aids the school in adequately presenting the school history. The school record is often the basis upon which the Court makes its plan for providing a program which will work to the advantage of all persons concerned.

Characteristics of an Effective Cumulative Record System.

A good cumulative record system:

1. Consists of items significant to all-round development of the student.
2. Shows trends in the individual's development.

3. Offers information moaningful to teacheis.

4. Furnishes data for every student, not for problem cases only.

5. Reflects the objectives of the educational program.

6. Presents information in such a way that growth data are consistent and comparable.

7. Involves a minimum of confusion during installation and operation.

8. Facilitates filing and using.

9. Provides information for teachers in easily understandable form.

10. Lends itself to easy and accurate reproduction for:
   a. teacher use.
   b. transcripts.

11. Involves a minimum of confusion or clerical work for the teacher.

Development of Cumulative Record Forms.

Several school districts have developed their own cumulative record systems. This has the advantage of providing an opportunity for teachers and administrators to work together in studying growth and development of boys and girls, and ways of recording data about them. Such a system should be adapted to local needs.

Certain cautions should be pointed out in the development of a local record system. One is the need for time. At least a year of committee work is desirable in order to develop such a plan.

The following steps in the development of a record system were listed by a school district which completed such a project:

1. Organize a cumulative record committee composed of teachers and administrators representing each school level.

2. Study the kind and amount of information which should be recorded.

3. Analyze records now in use to determine their strengths and weaknesses.

4. Examine cumulative records from other school districts and educational organizations for suggestions.

5. Develop preliminary record forms adapted to local needs.

6. Criticize tentative forms by cumulative record committees and by personnel responsible for health, curriculum and guidance.

7. Revise tentative forms.

8. Present revised forms to groups of teachers and administrators for constructive criticism.

9. Incorporate their suggestions into revised forms.

10. Prepare mimeographed copies to be submitted to as many teachers and administrators as possible for further criticism.

11. Make trial recordings of data for typical cases.

12. Revise in accordance with teacher recommendations and with experience derived from actual trial.

Adoption of a Published Cumulative Folder.

Several excellent cumulative record systems have been prepared for publication on a state-wide or national scale. One of these is the "California Cumulative Record for Junior and Senior High Schools."[2]   This form was designed by a

---

[2]Distributed by Dr. Harold B. Brooks (Long Beach Public Schools), Chairman of the Committee on Cumulative Records of the California Secondary School Principals' Association.

committee of secondary school administrators. It may be used in conjunction with the "California Cumulative Guidance Record for Elementary Schools."[3]

Adoption of such published folders may be advantageous in a school district because they provide a uniform approach to the study of children and to the recording of similar data by teachers and administrators throughout a large area such as the state or county.

Cautions.

Certain cautions need to be pointed out in connection with the introduction of such a record. The following suggestions are offered:

1. Some of the steps involved in faculty planning for setting up a local cumulative record system are applicable in adapting a published record system.

2. The initiation may be extended over a period of three years by introducing the form into the seventh and tenth grades, or over a period of two years by introducing it in the seventh, ninth and eleventh grades.

3. Data already recorded need not be copied on the new folder as the current form may be placed in the Basic Folder so that it will be complete.

4. A record system needs to be introduced gradually so that the burden of recording will not fall too heavily on any teacher at any time.

5. The counselor and teacher should be relieved of the clerical and routine aspects of record-keeping so that they can concentrate on the professional phase of recording and using data.

---

[3]Prepared by the Cumulative Records Committee, California State Supervisors Association. Published by A. Carlisle & Company, 135 Post Street, San Francisco 8, California.

Summary.

A cumulative record system is a plan for recording, filing and using information essential to the guidance of students. Such records are recognized as essential instruments for guidance in the modern school. An important criterion of a good cumulative record system is its provision for recording data significant in the all-round development of the student. This will include information about his health and physical development, home and family background, curricular experiences, aptitude and achievement, personal and social adjustment.

Suggested References.

Allen, Wendell C., *Cumulative Pupil Records.* New York: Teachers College, Columbia University, 1943.

Individual Inventory in Guidance Programs in Secondary Schools. United States Office of Education, Vocational Division, Bulletin No. 215; Washington, D. C.: Superintendent of Documents, 1941.

Ruch, G. M., and Segel, David, *Minimum Essentials of the Individual Inventory in Guidance.* United States Office of Education, Vocational Division, Bulletin No. 202; Washington, D. C.: Superintendent of Documents, 1938.

Segel, David, *Nature and Use of the Cumulative Record.* United States Office of Education, Bulletin, No. 3; Washington, D. C.: Superintendent of Documents, 1938.

Strang, Ruth, *Every Teacher's Records.* New York: Teachers College, Columbia University, 1936.

Traxler, Arthur E., "Cumulative Test Records: Their Nature and Uses," *Educational and Psychological Measurement*, 1:323-340, October, 1941.

_____*Techniques of Guidance.* New York: Harper and Brothers, 1945. Pp. 215-234.

CHAPTER III

TECHNIQUES FOR THE ADMINISTRATIVE USE OF GUIDANCE DATA

The part the superintendent and principal can play in organizing and maintaining an effective guidance program is outlined in this chapter under the following four headings:

1. Responsibility of the Superintendent and Principal.

2. Suggested Functions, Qualifications and Preparation of Personnel.

3. Administrative Policies and Practices Involving Use of Guidance Data for Promotion and Special Placement.

4. Using Guidance Data to Improve Curricular Offerings.

SECTION A. RESPONSIBILITY OF THE SUPERINTENDENT AND PRINCIPAL.

The administrator's role in guidance is a vital one because guidance is an integral part of the total school program. The course of study, master schedule, class size and teacher load, number of periods of teaching and counseling per teacher, planning of the testing program, developing appropriate reports, forms and cumulative records,—all of these and many other phases of the school program tie in with guidance services, and all are directly or indirectly the responsibility of the administrator.

Also involved in the establishment and operation of a guidance program is the coordination of the efforts of all members of the staff as well as the selection and induction of new members. Furthermore, guidance involves relationships with community organizations such as service clubs, Chambers of Commerce, churches, Boy Scouts and Y.M.C.A. The guidance program must be interpreted to the Board of Education and to the community in order to assure adequate understanding and support. Who, better than the superintendent, principal, or top assistants, can plan, advise, make decisions and carry or delegate responsibility in these matters? Important as are the classroom teacher and the specialist in a guidance program, each will be ineffectual unless the administrator does his part.

What the Administrator Can Do to Improve the Guidance Program.

Administrators of Los Angeles Couny school districts have been quite successful in the development of guidance programs. The chief reasons for their success appear to be:

1. Development of a guidance philosophy in cooperation with the staff.
2. Assignment of responsibility for planning and administering a guidance program.
3. Cooperative consideration of problems in developing and operating a guidance program.
4. Provision of adequate facilities for guidance.
5. Utilization of available County and State resources.
6. Support of and continuous interest in the guidance program.

Further elaboration may be made under each of the above:

1. Develop a guidance philosophy in cooperation with the staff. By this is meant stimulating the administrative staff to consider the place of guidance in a modern secondary school, the physical, mental, social and emotional characteristics of boys and girls, and the best ways of providing for their needs. Through discussion

a staff may develop a philosophy which will direct the guidance program. The following principles might be developed or accepted by a faculty:

a. Teachers, counselors, administrators and others responsible for guidance will look upon all guidance activities as means of adjusting the school's program to the needs of individual students.

b. Guidance should be extended to **all** students in the school, not limited to those who are obviously maladjusted.

c. Guidance should endeavor to make a student increasingly able to direct his own activities wisely.

d. Guidance workers need special training.

e. Guidance must involve the use of carefully collected data.

f. Guidance is a continuous process, not simply a service to be offered at certain grade levels, or at critical points in a student's career.

g. The guidance program should be articulated for all students from kindergarten through high school and junior college.

2. Assign responsibility for planning and administering a guidance program.

In the larger schools or school districts the administrator is too busy to work out the details of a guidance program, or to supervise a program which is already under way. This responsibility is usually delegated to someone on the staff on a full-time or part-time basis depending upon the size of the school.

Three representative types of organization for guidance are presented in chart form in Appendix A. Chart I indicates a possible organization in which responsibility for guidance is centered in the counselor; Chart II when responsibility is centered in the teacher;

and Chart III when responsibility is centered in the director of guidance.

The guidance director should be a person who has had considerable training in guidance, psychology and statistics, in addition to successful experience as a teacher or administrator. Occupational experience in addition to teaching is also recommended.

The qualifications of a guidance worker have been considered by a statewide committee of administrative guidance personnel under the chairmanship of Dr. Emery Stoops, formerly Coordinator of Research and Guidance, Los Angeles County Schools.[1] This report entitled "Suggested Functions, Qualifications and Preparation of Guidance Personnel" is presented in Section B of this chapter.

3. Consider problems in developing a guidance program. The guidance director with the advice of the administrator will need to consider such problems as:

a. What is the most appropriate program for this school or school district, in terms of the type of community served, the number of students and teachers, the financial resources of the district, the vocational and educational opportunities for students after graduation?

b. How large a guidance staff is needed? Which staff members are best qualified to serve as full-time or part-time counselors? How can the guidance program utilize the talents of all members of the staff? What will be the place of the classroom teacher in counseling? of the specialist? the vice-principal? the dean? the principal?

c. What use should be made of such devices for col-

---

[1]Los Angeles County Superintendent of Schools, "Suggested Functions, Qualifications and Preparation of Guidance Personnel." (Bulletin No. 15000; Los Angeles 12: Division of Research and Guidance, July, 1946.)

lecting student information as the testing program, the interview, cumulative records, observation and anecdotal records, autobiography, questionnaire, case study and others?

d. How may the information about students be used most effectively in determining the age-grade situation in the school? in securing the optimum placement for each student?

e. How can guidance data be used to determine the strengths and weaknesses of the instructional program and to make adjustments?

f. How may guidance data be used most effectively in such group situations as the core course or home room, elective courses, extracurricular activities, school assemblies, special guidance events?

g. How may counseling be made more effective in dealing with the problems of physical health, mental health, personal-social, educational and vocational plans and other problems which puzzle students?

h. What techniques will prove most effective in stimulating professional growth of all members of the staff in activities essential to guidance?

i. What techniques should be used to interpret the guidance program to the community?

j. How can the staff evaluate the strengths and weaknesses of the entire guidance program and take steps toward improvement?

4. Provide adequate physical facilities for guidance.

The problem of where to find adequate office space for counselors faces many administrators. This problem has been particularly acute where the buildings were constructed years before modern personnel practices were introduced and where increasing school enrollments have made it necessary to utilize all available

been available for counselors' offices. In those districts where building programs are being planned, however, the following suggestions for counseling facilities may be helpful.

a. Offices for counselors should be in the same suite as the administrative offices.

b. Offices for counselors should be close to the nurses' and doctors' offices.

c. Adequate, well-lighted space for clerical workers should be provided adjacent to the counselors' offices.

d. In addition to counselors' offices, a small conference room should be provided for individual testing, interviews with parents and the like.

e. A larger conference room, class-size, should adjoin the suite. This will provide space for group testing, large conferences, staff meetings.

f. Each counselor's office should have at least 150 square feet of floor space.

g. The waiting room for the personnel office should have a minimum of 150 square feet, if there is one counselor's office. With the addition of each counselor's office, an additional 50 square feet should be added to the waiting room.

h. Personnel offices should include storage and filing space, preferably built-in closets, bookcases, cupboards and bulletin boards.

i. Office equipment should include typewriters, mimeograph machine, calculating machine. In the larger city districts an electric test scoring machine may be needed in order to reduce the amount of teacher time spent in scoring.

j. Counselors' offices should be sound-proof and well lighted.

k. Office furnishings should include large movable desks, with space for a work table, and several chairs.

The secondary school administrator who is able to provide some if not all of these physical facilities for guidance will improve the effectiveness of the guidance worker.

5. Utilize available County and State resources.

Experienced consultants are available from both the Office of the Los Angeles County Superintendent of Schools and the California State Department of Education.

a. Services of the Office of the Los Angeles County Superintendent of Schools.

Representatives of the Divisions of Elementary Education, Secondary Education, Attendance and Child Welfare, Audio-Visual Education, Trade and Industrial Education and Health and Physical Education are available for assistance in dealing with specific problems in their field.

Coordinators of the Division of Research and Guidance are assigned to offer the following types of guidance service to secondary schools of Los Angeles County:

(1) Assisting secondary school districts in planning and conducting educational and psychological surveys of aptitude, ability, achievement and adjustment, and in setting up an effective cumulative record system to facilitate guidance functions.

(2) Consulting with administrators, teachers and counselors concerning the results of both individual and group tests, and their implications for student guidance and evaluation of the school program, and cooperating with the Division of Secondary Education in discussing

group test results and adjustments which may be made.

(3) Conducting individual psychological case studies of student problems, such as: reading difficulty, mental retardation, personality or speech problems, and interpreting the findings in conference with the school staff.

(4) Assisting with the in-service training of teachers in research and guidance techniques.

(5) Preparing bulletins, reports and bibliographies regarding research and guidance findings and procedures.

(6) Assembling, compiling and distributing data for purposes of guidance.

(7) Assisting school districts in relation to the following aspects of vocational guidance: planning career day; conducting community occupational surveys; collecting, organizing and using occupational information; preparing and teaching vocational units and planning placement and follow-up procedures.

(8) Interpreting the guidance program to teacher, parent and lay groups by means of institute programs, study groups and professional meetings.

b. Services of the Bureau of Occupational Information and Guidance, California State Department of Education. The Chief of the Bureau of Occupational Information and Guidance and his assistant are available on call to offer the following services:[2]

(1) Preparing material for distribution to individuals, schools and other agencies, describing

---

[2]California State Department of Education, *Vocational Education in California*. (Bulletin XIV, No. 4; Sacramento: Bureau of Vocational Education, October, 1945), Pp. 52-53.

successful studies, surveys and investigations in occupational information and guidance.

(2) Working with schools in determining and recommending the equipment, library materials, and other supplementary supplies and facilities that will be needed to make a program of occupational information and guidance effective in the several school units.

(3) Consulting with school superintendents, principals and supervisors who desire information regarding establishment of programs of occupational information and guidance and aiding in the organization of such programs as have been approved by the local authorities.

(4) Aiding in the development of the program by making services of a speaker available to civic groups, parent-teacher organizations, teachers' meetings and conferences, setting forth the basic principles of a sound and effective program of occupational information and guidance.

(5) Promoting occupational information and guidance programs by working in close cooperation with existing agencies, public and private, which contribute to the advancement of the various objectives of the program.

(6) Studying means of improving the professional preparation of teacher-counselors or other persons who are designated in individual schools to carry on programs of guidance. Promoting means of in-service training of teachers and counselors, as well as the work of teacher-training institutions in guidance.

(7) Conducting, in cooperation with local authorities, group conferences and meetings for the

purpose of improving local programs of occupational information and guidance.

6. Stimulate continuous interest in the guidance program. Another reason for the success of guidance programs in Los Angeles County is each administrator's continued interest in supporting guidance services. Even though the guidance philosophy, training of the staff, and guidance procedures are praiseworthy, the guidance program will lose its force and direction unless the administrator shows continuous interest in the work being accomplished.

The final chapter of the handbook entitled "Appraisal of the Guidance Program" will assist the administrator in determining more easily the strengths and weaknesses of the guidance services in his school. An occasional conference with the guidance director, a word of approval or of constructive criticism, will vitalize and inspire the entire staff.

Suggested References.

California State Department of Education, *Vocational Education in California*. Bulletin XIV, No. 4; Sacramento: Bureau of Vocational Education, October, 1945.

Jones, Arthur J., *Principles of Guidance*. New York: McGraw-Hill Book Company, 1945. Pp. 74-77.

Los Angeles County Superintendent of Schools, "Suggested Functions, Qualifications and Preparation of Guidance Personnel." Bulletin No. 15000; Los Angeles 12: Division of Research and Guidance, July, 1946.

SECTION B. SUGGESTED FUNCTIONS, QUALIFICATIONS AND PREPARATION OF GUIDANCE PERSONNEL.

The administrator must delegate responsibility for guidance services to members of his staff. The guidance program will be successful in the degree to which personnel are qualified and trained. The following report is based upon a monograph prepared by members of the Sub-Committee of the State Guidance Committee of the California State Supervisors Association. The report sets forth desirable functions, qualifications and preparation for guidance workers.

This report on the functions, qualifications and preparation of guidance personnel has been prepared to serve the following purposes:

1. To assist school administrators in selecting qualified guidance workers.

2. To assist teacher-training institutions in developing well-rounded training programs for guidance workers.

3. To assist prospective applicants in planning professional training programs.

4. To stimulate further development of effective guidance services.

Functions of Guidance Personnel.

The functions of guidance personnel may appropriately be divided into two major categories: (1) direct services to students, and (2) additional services required in a coordinated program.

1. Direct Services to Students.
   a. Studying the needs, interests, abilities, achievements, aptitudes and personality of each counselee.
   b. Informing students of the opportunities open to them in the school and community, making use of group methods, written materials, visual aids and interviews.
   c. Assisting each counselee to plan a long-term program in harmony with his potentialities and opportunities.

d. Assisting each counselee to plan a specific course and activity program for each semester.

e. Preparing and keeping up-to-date the cumulative counseling records of each counselee.

f. Counseling with each student who comes for help with personal, social, vocational or educational problems.

g. Informing teachers at the beginning of each semester of significant facts about each student, thus enabling the teacher to do a better job of teaching individuals.

h. Analyzing the achievement records of each counselee and initiating interviews, follow-up and remedial procedures where indicated.

i. Diagnosing special cases through psychological tests, home visits and other appropriate methods; bringing the total resources of school and community to the assistance of those individuals.

j. Providing an effective occupational information, placement and follow-up service for students and graduates.

k. Meeting with parents to discuss the progress and promise of individual counselees.

2. Additional Services Required in a Coordinated Program.

a. Organizing, coordinating and supervising the total guidance program within a school.

b. Collecting, interpreting and presenting research data needed for the continuous evaluation and revision of the total educational program.

c. Cooperating with other members of the school staff in interpreting the educational program to the community.

d. Preparing class and school data for use in scheduling, grouping and promotion.

e. Coordinating youth services in the school with all community guidance agencies.

f. Stimulating and developing professional growth activities for all staff members.

Recommended Personal Qualifications of Guidance Workers.

1. Exhibit willingness to work "beyond the call of duty."
2. Maintain consistently a friendly, approachable manner.
3. Have a high degree of emotional stability.
4. Maintain objectivity in human relationships.
5. Evidence interest in continuous professional improvement.

Recommended Experience for Guidance Workers.

1. Two or more years of successful teaching.
2. Vocational experience other than teaching—experience in social case work and in personnel management is particularly relevant, but wide job experience is important.
3. Participation and leadership in professional and community activities.

Preparation of Guidance Personnel.

A functioning guidance program requires the participation of guidance workers at different levels of specialization. Suggestions for the preparation of such personnel are given below.

1. Teachers should have insight into guidance problems and should possess what might be called a guidance point of view. Since the guidance functions stated above are pertinent to the elementary as well as to the secondary school, it is important that teacher-training institutions for all classifications of teachers make provision for including sufficient materials to give all teach-

ers an insight into the nature of the needs of individuals, and the general organization and scope of school and community guidance services.

2. Counselors.
   a. Four major areas of training may be recommended:
      (1) Understanding of the organization, purposes and function of a guidance program.
      (2) Understanding of and skill in appraising individual abilities, interests and needs.
      (3) Understanding of social and vocational opportunities in the state and community.
      (4) Understanding of techniques of individual counseling.
   b. Recommended courses are as follows:
      (1) Growth and Development of the Child.
      (2) Educational Psychology.
      (3) Social Psychology.
      (4) Educational Tests and Measurements.
      (5) Methods of Social Investigation and Case Study.
      (6) Elementary Research Methods.
      (7) Principles and Techniques of Guidance and Counseling.
      (8) Mental Hygiene.
      (9) Educational and Vocational Guidance.
      (10) Supervised Experience in Counseling.
3. Specialists in Guidance. Each school system and, in many cases, each large school needs a fully qualified specialist to serve as the director or the coordinator of the total guidance program. In addition to the above courses, the specialist needs intensive training in the following areas:
   a. Advanced Educational Psychology.
   b. Clinical Psychology.
   c. Psychological Testing.

d. Principles of Psychiatry.
e. Advanced Research Methods.
f. Principles of Sociology and Social Case Work.
g. Economics and Labor Problems.
h. Vocational Education.
i. Externeship in Clinical Counseling.

Sub-Committee Members who Prepared the Above Report:

Dr. Richmond D. Barbour, Director of Guidance, San Diego City Schools.

Dr. Charlotte Elmott, Director of Guidance, Santa Barbara City Schools.

Dr. D. Welty Lefever, Professor of Education, University of Southern California.

Dr. Ina K. Dillon, Elementary Training School, University of California at Los Angeles.

Dr. Jessica Miller Haskell, Psychologist, Long Beach City Schools.

Dr. A. Elwood Adams, Principal, Stephens Junior High School, Long Beach City Schools.

Dr. Margaret Bennett, Director of Guidance, Pasadena City Schools.

Dr. Norman Scharer, Principal, Alhambra High School.

Dr. J. Paul Leonard, President, San Francisco State College.

Dr. H. B. McDaniel, formerly Chief, Bureau of Occupational Information and Guidance, State Department of Education; at present Associate Professor of Education, Stanford University.

Dr. Harry Smallenburg, Director of Research and Guidance, Los Angeles County Superintendent of School Office.

Dr. Emery Stoops, Chairman, formerly Coordinator of Research and Guidance; at present Administrative Assistant, Los Angeles County Superintendent of Schools Office.

SECTION C. ADMINISTRATIVE POLICIES AND PRACTICES INVOLVING USE OF GUIDANCE DATA FOR PROMOTION AND SPECIAL PLACEMENT.[3]

This section is designed to assist administrators in placing students in the grades or groups in which they can achieve the greatest success. The discussion has been organized into three parts: (1) suggestions for promotional procedures, (2) individual and clinical study as a basis for special promotion, and (3) adjusted program for specially promoted students. Several suggestions are made under each of these headings.

Suggested Promotional Procedures.

These suggestions apply to two types of students: those attending Los Angeles County Schools prior to time for special promotion and those students from out-of-state and out-of-district.

Students Attending Los Angeles County Schools Prior to Time for Special Promotion.

Suggestion 1. Students of normal mental capacity should ordinarily progress through the grades at the rate of one grade per year.[4]

In practice, this means that students of average intelligence should move through the grades in groups of similarly aged students by being promoted one grade each year. It also requires the establishment and acceptance of certain age-grade relationships as "normal."

Suggestion 2. Students who are limited in mental capacity and learning ability may be allowed to become a year retarded for convenience of instruction.

---

[3]Approved, on Executive Council recommendation, by the Los Angeles County High School Principals' Association, June, 1946.

[4]Los Angeles County Superintendent of Schools, "Statement of Elementary School Promotion Policy" (Bulletin No. 8103; Los Angeles, 12: Division of Research and Guidance, 1940).

This means that some students, because of their intellectual limitations, may be expected to have difficulty in typical classroom situations. They will benefit, therefore, by being allowed to become one year retarded. This adjustment is made to facilitate classroom teaching and to afford those students increased opportunity for success which will result in a feeling of adequacy and satisfaction in learning.

Suggestion 3. Students of superior mental capacity or learning ability may be allowed to become one year accelerated so that they may be given work suited to their capacity and needs.

This acceleration of gifted students is often desirable as it allows the presentation of a more challenging program and the placement in a more congenial social group.

Caution. Acceleration or retardation of more than one year should be rare and should be permitted only in instances where it is definitely in the interest of the student, because of unusual handicap or ability. This means that careful individual study should be made to determine whether such special placement will improve the student's adjustment.

Administrators should survey their schools periodically to determine the age-grade status of their students in relation to their mental ability.

Best Time for Special Promotion.

If it is anticipated that a special promotion might be warranted, the logical time should be a year prior to the entrance of a student into a higher level or different school.

For instance, special promotions should be considered in such critical grades as:

1. Eighth grade in a three-year junior high school.
2. Ninth grade in a four-year junior high school.

Reasons for making special promotions in these critical grades follow:

1. A handicap is placed on a student if he misses the last year in school with his regular class. He should be able to adjust to the new school more readily as a member of his own class group.

2. He will need that last year for preparation and orientation for the advanced school experience similar to that received by the whole class.

3. A student who is limited in his ability to learn as rapidly and efficiently as the normal or gifted will definitely be handicapped by missing the last year in his present school situation.

This plan, then, will not require any regularly enrolled student to miss the last year of his present school experience because of special promotion. Suggestions for promotion of students of varying levels of ability are given in detail later in this section.

Adoption of the "Promotional Policy for Elementary Schools" by the Los Angeles County Board of Education in 1940 resulted in the acceptance of certain normal age ranges for specific grades. These age-grade relationships are presented in the table below:

NORMAL AGE RANGES FOR GRADES 5 - 12

(As disclosed by research and test data compiled over a period of more than ten years)

Gr. 5	Gr. 6	Gr. 7	Gr. 8	Gr. 9	Gr. 10	Gr. 11	Gr. 12
10-6	11-7	12-8	13-6	14-5	15-3	16-3	17-2
to	to	to	to	to	to	to	to
11-6	12-7	13-5	14-4	15-2	16-2	17-1	18-2

Figures represent years and months

1. Placement of Normal Pupils and Students.

   a. Applying Suggestion 1 to the above range, pupils of normal ability in the fifth grade who are chronologically from 10 years 6 months to 11 years 6 months of age, are correctly placed in their grade.

   b. Applying Suggestion 1, again, to the above range, pupils of normal ability in the sixth grade who are chronologically from 11 years 7 months to 12 years 7 months of age, are correctly placed in their grade.

2. Special Placement of Slow Learners.

   a. Applying Suggestion 2 to this range, a slow learner, at the beginning of the fifth grade, might be considered for special promotion to the sixth grade if he has reached the age of 12 years and 8 months.

   b. Again applying Suggestion 2, a slow learner, at the beginning of the eighth grade, might be considered for special promotion into the ninth grade when he has reached the age of 15 years and 3 months.

3. Special Placement of Superior Students.

   a. Applying Suggestion 3, a superior student, at the beginning of the seventh grade, might be considered for special promotion into the eighth grade when he has reached the age of 12 years and 8 months.

   b. Again applying Suggestion 3, a superior student, at the beginning of the ninth grade, might be considered for special promotion into the tenth grade when he has reached the age of 14 years and 5 months.

4. Students from Out-of-State or Out-of-District.

   a. Many students transfer to Los Angeles County from **out-of-state** or **out-of-district.** Study of the age-grade status may reveal that such students are not adequately placed for most effective learning.

   b. Each of these new students should be considered individually.

    c. This consideration should be taken into account as soon as possible after enrollment in the new school situation, even though the logical time for special promotion may have passed.

Individual and Clinical Study as a Basis for Special Promotion.

All special promotion cases should be given individual study.

1. The cumulative record data for each student should be reviewed carefully, including:
   a. Mental age and I.Q. (Language and Non-Language).
   b. Achievement grade placements, especially in reading and language.
   c. Comparison of achievement with capacity (expectancy).
   d. Physical maturity, stature and health.
   e. Personal-social adjustment.

2. All factors should be studied cooperatively by personnel from each school concerned, where two schools are involved in the special promotion, such as: (elementary and junior high schools; elementary and high schools; junior and senior high schools).
   The following personnel may be involved:
   a. Principal of each school, or his representative.
   b. School personnel such as nurse, physician, counselor, home teacher or social worker, attendance officer or others who have information about the case.
   c. Psychologist or Coordinator of Research and Guidance serving each school.

3. Final decision regarding special promotion should be reached on the basis of all factors involved. The promotion placement should be based upon a cooperative decision by the principals of both schools. This cooperative decision should result in the most advantageous placement for the individual student.

Adjustment Program for Specially Promoted Students.

1. Psychological characteristics of slow-learning students and of superior students.

   In order to provide a program for specially promoted students, the administrator will need to know the psychological characteristics of slow-learning and superior students. Some of these characteristics are listed below.

   a. Some psychological characteristics of certain slow-learning students:
      (1) Short attention span.
      (2) Slow reaction time.
      (3) Poor memory.
      (4) Few successful school experiences, with history of repeated failures.
      (5) More effective learning by visual impressions and manipulative contacts than by auditory impressions.
      (6) Likely to have physical as well as psychological handicaps.
      (7) Concrete learning rather than abstract learning.
      (8) Inadequate verbalization.
      (9) Poor sense of direction and orientation.
      (10) Inferior coordination.
      (11) Lack of initiative.

   b. Some psychological characteristics of certain superior students:
      (1) Quick reaction time.
      (2) Good memory.
      (3) Fine reasoning ability.
      (4) Self-direction.
      (5) Notable qualities of leadership.
      (6) Exceptional verbal ability and language development.
      (7) Abstract thinking ability.

(8)   Good coordination.
(9)   Logical planning ability.
(10) Concentration and attention.
(11) Creative ability.

2. The foregoing principles and policies pre-suppose that
    the school in which a specially promoted student will
    be enrolled will provide a program that is flexible
    enough to meet individual capacities, interests and
    needs, as to:

    a. Adequate curriculum offerings that will capitalize
       upon assets and minimize liabilities.
    b. Enrichment of curriculum and leadership opportuni-
       ties for superior students.
    c. Developmental classes for slow learners.
    d. Corrective classes for remedial cases.

Summary.

The implications for educational adjustment of specially
promoted students into a new situation are very important,
and secondary school administrators and guidance personnel
will do well to study them carefully in order to provide adequate programs that will meet individual capacities and interests.

Suggested References:

Los Angeles City Superintendent of Schools, *Guidance in Elementary
Schools.* School Publication No. 398; Los Angeles 12: Los Angeles
City Schools, 1944.

Los Angeles County Superintendent of Schools, "Statement of Elementary School Promotion Policy." Bulletin No. 8103; Los Angeles
12: Division of Research and Guidance, 1940.

University of the State of New York, *Pupil Progress in Elementary
Schools of New York State.* Bulletin No. 1297; Albany: New York
State Education Department, July, 1945.

SECTION D. USING GUIDANCE DATA TO IMPROVE CURRICULAR OFFERINGS.

Administrative Use of Guidance Data in Improving the Curriculum.

Earlier publications on guidance placed emphasis on ways of helping students to adjust to the educational program of the school. Recently the emphasis has shifted to the point of view that the curriculum and methods of instruction must be adapted to student interests, abilities and needs.

The more effectively the educational program is adjusted to student needs, the fewer will be the number of student problems which indicate need for guidance such as failure, misbehavior, truancy and excessive requests for work permits. In order for the administrator to develop educational programs adjusted to needs of students, guidance data need to be available and utilized.

The terms "curriculum" and "educational program" may be regarded as virtually synonymous and as consisting of all of the planned opportunities for educational experiences provided under the direction of the school.

Development of a functional educational program for individual students as well as for groups, necessitates using several kinds of guidance data in order to obtain information about student interests, aptitudes, capacities, skills and proficiencies, social and home backgrounds and personal-social problems.

Using Guidance Data for Individualizing the Curriculum.

For working purposes, individualization of the curriculum can be defined as taking place whenever certain students are given experiences differing from those of other members of a class or organized instructional group. Guidance data should be utilized. Factors which necessitate that much of the curriculum and teaching be individualized are:

1. Differences in rate of physical growth and development.
2. Differences in capacity, achievement and interest.
3. Differences in social and emotional adjustment.

In order to determine the way in which the students' learning experiences need to be individualized, the following types of information and data are needed:

1. Aptitudes, achievements and interests.
2. Personal-social adjustment to school, home, community and the like.
3. Cultural-economic status of home and family background.
4. History of school progress from early elementary grades through high school.
5. Health, physical growth and maturity.

The methods and techniques for gathering data are described in Chapter II, "Techniques for Collecting and Recording Guidance Data."

Using Guidance Data to Develop Varied Curricular Offerings for Groups.

A functional curriculum for groups of students has the following characteristics:

1. It provides experiences and knowledges obtained through the curriculum, which reflect the more urgent aspirations and desires of youth.
2. It provides experiences which are related to the major areas of life in the community.
3. It provides experiences which enable students to develop skills necessary to participate effectively in life at home, in school, in the community and in the nation.

Guidance data for developing a curriculum adapted to needs of students should be utilized by:

1. Administrators, curriculum directors, counselors and consultants in planning the general scope and sequence of the curriculum.

2. Curriculum committees in developing content and teaching activities for units of work and courses of study.
3. Classroom teachers in planning learning experiences and activities for students.

Adapting the Curriculum to Meet Individual Differences.

1. Providing optional units of purposeful work or study within a subject or course, units which involve student participation in planning.
2. Permitting each student to choose topics or subjects within his or her range of experience and interest. Such topics should be related to the general areas of the curriculum outlined in the course of study.
3. Providing opportunities for students to select and participate in school activities along lines of their own interests and needs.
4. Planning work so that assignments are commensurate with individual student capacities and allowing time to complete them.
5. Furnishing classrooms with sets of books of varying levels of reading difficulty.
6. Providing for small groups within each classroom according to interest and ability.
7. Providing opportunities for students to take elective courses organized for groups of students with similar needs and interests.

Adapting the Curriculum to Meet Common Needs and Problems.

There are certain types of common experiences which are particularly important for all students. Among these are experiences which develop skills and values essential to daily living.

Guidance data are essential in determining when instruction should be provided to groups of students with regard to such problems as:

1. How to develop personal attractiveness.
2. How to get along with others.
3. How to conduct oneself in social gatherings.
4. How to get along with one's family.
5. How to understand the purpose and function of sex.
6. How to select a vocation and prepare for it.
7. How to become an effective citizen.

Guidance data can be useful in identifying and helping to solve problems which condition students' progress through school and adjustment to the society in which they live.

Summary.

Guidance data should be utilized in order to plan an effective educational program. Certain types of information and data are needed in order to individualize the curriculum for all students and to make the curriculum suit needs of class groups. Guidance data should be utilized by all persons who have a part in the development of the curriculum and direction of the instruction. Periodic checks or an evaluation should be made to appraise the use of guidance data in developing the educational program.

Suggested References.

Johnson, B. Lamar, Editor, *General Education in the American High School*. Chicago: Scott, Foresman and Company, 1942.

Mackenzie, Gordon H., "Implications for Teachers and Counselors," *Forty-Third Yearbook of the National Society for the Study of Education*, Part I. Chicago: University of Chicago Bookstore, 1944.

Meek (Stolz), Lois H., et al., *Personal-Social Development of Boys and Girls*. New York: Progressive Education Association, 1940.

Sheviakov, George, "The Necessity of Understanding the Adolescent As a Basis for Curriculum and Guidance," *Journal of the National Association of Deans of Women*. 5:7-12, October, 1941.

CHAPTER IV

GROUP TECHNIQUES FOR UTILIZING GUIDANCE DATA

Purposes in Using Group Guidance Techniques.

Group guidance techniques have an important place in the modern secondary school because they:

1. Conserve teacher time and energy.
2. Help students to gain more guidance information by means of exploratory courses and the like.
3. Assist the school in building desirable attitudes by creating an awareness of certain basic ideals of character.
4. Develop inter-personal skills by providing an opportunity to gain experience in using democratic processes.
5. Help create respect for group rules.
6. Lay a foundation for individual guidance.
7. Facilitate the handling of administrative detail of the school.
8. Stimulate and create interest in the school.
9. Train students to be intelligent followers of democratically elected officers.
10. Provide experience in the wise use of right-to-vote.

Importance of Cooperative Utilization of Guidance Data.

Every school is composed of three groups:

1. Administration.
2. Instructional staff.
3. Student body.

94

The responsibility of the administration is to provide satisfactory conditions for group guidance.

The teacher's greatest contribution in group guidance can be made as part of his regular classroom activities, not in a special period set apart for guidance purposes. The teacher will need to readjust the emphasis from subject matter goals to student development objectives.

The application of democratic processes in student activities is a desirable means of group guidance. Channeling the great vigor and enthusiasm of youth into constructive experiences will result in greater achievement in school. Wholehearted student support of the total school program is necessary if the group needs of students are to be met adequately.

Thus, the best utilization of guidance data is found where administrators, teachers and students work in close cooperation in securing, interpreting and applying these data. This procedure will more adequately prepare all students for group cooperation in later life.

Using Group Techniques to Guide Youth

Group techniques for utilizing guidance data fall into four general classifications: (1) core curriculum or guidance classes; (2) electives and special classes; (3) extracurricular activities, and (4) special guidance events. The several group guidance techniques under the four general classifications are listed below:

1. Core curriculum and guidance classes.
    a. Core curriculum courses.
        (1) Integration of subject matter as a means of developing personal and social competency.
        (2) Creation of interest in community problems.
        (3) Discovery of student assets and liabilities.

      (4) Stimulation and development of interests, aptitudes and achievement.

      (5) Educational and vocational planning.

      (6) Adjustment to school personnel and facilities.

      (7) Provision for better individual adjustment.

b. Homerooms.

      (1) Organization to promote democratic relationships in the homeroom.

      (2) Provision for better appraisal of personal assets and liabilities.

      (3) Procurement of information about opportunities: educational, vocational, personal - social and civic.

      (4) Participation in development of social skills.

      (5) Stimulation of interest in extracurricular activities.

      (6) Consideration of ways to improve the school as a community.

c. Orientation courses.

      (1) Survey of school plant facilities.

      (2) Study of rules and regulations.

      (3) Acquaintance with school customs and traditions.

      (4) Knowledge of the school's place as a community institution.

      (5) Acquaintance with school personnel.

      (6) Information about school services available through library, student store, cafeteria and the like.

      (7) Perspective of the school's educational offerings.

      (8) Instruction in how to study in high school and in college.

      (9) Provision for practice in getting along with people.

d. Occupational and educational information units.

    (1) Appraisal of self with respect to vocational assets.

    (2) Appraisal of occupational opportunities available.

    (3) Study of how to secure jobs.

    (4) Information about how to succeed on the job.

    (5) Study of training necessary to advance within a job.

    (6) Information about graduation requirements.

    (7) Comparison of college entrance requirements.

    (8) Consideration of specific courses that train for selected occupations.

2. Elective and special classes.

  a. Leadership classes.

    (1) Information about the qualities of a leader.

    (2) Consideration of responsibilities involved in leadership.

    (3) Instruction in how to follow as well as lead.

    (4) Survey of school leadership opportunities.

    (5) Relation of school success to leadership ability.

  b. Practical arts courses.

    (1) Training in common skills.

    (2) Appreciation of the importance of mechanical occupations.

    (3) Survey of jobs requiring training provided by the school.

    (4) Stimulation of interest in practical arts.

    (5) Appraisal of aptitudes and mechanical and household activities.

  c. Exploratory courses.

    (1) Development of vocational and avocational interests.

    (2) Information concerning further training in chosen fields.

OVER

       (3)   Acquisition of skills for home maintenance.

       (4)   Discovery and development of aptitudes.

   d. Special classes: journalism, music, art, drama, speech and others.

       (1)   Acquisition of hobbies.

       (2)   Enrichment of personal culture.

       (3)   Expansion of interests.

       (4)   Development of artistic and communicative ability.

       (5)   Cooperation with others through participation in art and communication.

       (6)   Training for worthy use of leisure time.

       (7)   Exploration of educational and vocational possibilities.

       (8)   Training for enriched home and community life.

3. Extracurricular activities.

   a. Athletic organizations.

       (1)   Development of an attitude of fair play.

       (2)   Stimulation of team loyalty.

       (3)   Encouragement of consideration for team members and supporters of opposing schools.

       (4)   Practice in taking hard knocks without complaint.

       (5)   Development of quick thinking and initiative.

       (6)   Training in following precise directions.

   b. Club activities.

       (1)   Provision for adolescent liking for group participation.

       (2)   Creation of an outlet for student enthusiasms.

       (3)   Stimulation of interest in school and community activities.

       (4)   Development of leadership.

       (5)   Provision for constructive use of spare time.

   c. Student body government.

      (1) Participation in democratic form of school government.

      (2) Development of leadership and followership.

      (3) Creation of a means to promote school loyalty.

      (4) Development of situations requiring initiative and responsibility.

      (5) Training for further participation in community government.

      (6) Building of favorable attitudes toward democratic processes.

4. Special guidance events.

  a. Field trips.

      (1) Provision of first-hand information.

      (2) Promotion of proper attitudes toward industry, government, scientific and cultural institutions.

      (3) Broadening of acquaintance with community activities and resources.

      (4) Stimulation of interest in near-by places.

      (5) Appreciation of local enterprises and products.

  b. Pre-enrollment orientation meetings or Freshman Day Program.

      (1) Information concerning next highest school grade.

      (2) Arousal of interest in advanced schooling.

      (3) Adjustment of individual interests and capacities to course offerings.

      (4) Development of loyalty to the program of the new school.

      (5) Orientation to requirements and opportunities at the new school.

      (6) Acquaintance with classmates and faculty personnel.

      (7) Directions to library, cafeteria, wash rooms and offices.

c. Career days (See "Suggestions for Career Days" Los Angeles County Superintendent of Schools Office, Research and Guidance Monograph No. 15075).

(1) Consideration of the place of jobs in community living.
(2) Presentation of facts about employment trends.
(3) First-hand information about specific jobs.
(4) Encouragement of closer student cooperation with school counselors.
(5) Motivation for subjects or courses which lead to jobs.
(6) Inspiration concerning opportunities in the vocational world of today.

d. Dramatic, speech, musical and art festivals.

(1) Development of artistic talents.
(2) Advancement of artistic appreciation.
(3) Selection of an artistic vocation.
(4) Development of self-confidence and feelings of success.
(5) Information concerning artistic preferences of community.

e. Exhibits.

(1) Practice in arranging models and objects.
(2) Appreciation for public likes and dislikes.
(3) Cooperation with classmates in selecting mechanical or household art objects for display.
(4) Cooperation on class products.
(5) Appreciation of precise workmanship.
(6) Development of interest in technical processes.

f. School assemblies.

(1) Appreciation of the importance of audience interests.
(2) Celebration of school triumphs.
(3) Arousal of school spirit and enthusiasm.

(4) Appreciation of the functions of the school.
(5) Development of audience behavior.
(6) Stimulation toward improved student morale.
(7) Practice in learning to listen.

Summary

Group techniques for utilizing guidance data in the modern school are important because they provide students with information and the opportunity to develop inter-personal skills, additional interests and practice in democratic activities. Group techniques save teacher time and facilitate administrative detail. The administration, instructional staff and student body should cooperate in setting up group guidance services, in improving group techniques in the classroom and in evaluating the outcomes. The four major techniques for utilizing guidance data are: (1) Core curriculum courses; (2) elective and special classes; (3) extracurricular activities, and (4) special guidance events.

Suggested References.

Bell, Howard M., *Matching Youth and Jobs.* Washington, D. C.: American Council on Education, 1940.

Dunsmoor, C. C., and Miller, L. M., *Guidance Methods for Teachers.* Scranton: International Book Company, 1942.

Edmonson, J. B., et al., *The Administration of the Modern Secondary School.* New York: The Macmillan Company, 1941.

Koos, Leonard V., et al., *Administering the Secondary School.* San Francisco: American Book Company, 1940.

Lefever, D. Welty, et al., *Principles and Techniques of Guidance.* New York: The Ronald Press Company, 1941.

Reed, Anna Y., *Guidance and Personnel Services in Education.* Ithaca, New York: Cornell University Press, 1944.

CHAPTER V

TECHNIQUES FOR TEACHER AND COUNSELOR USE OF GUIDANCE DATA

In this chapter techniques are suggested by means of which a classroom teacher and/or counselor may make use of guidance data. The chapter is divided into the following five sections:

Guiding Students Regarding Physical and Mental Health.
    Part I. Physical Health.
    Part II. Mental Health.

Guiding Students Regarding Personal-Social Problems.

The Counseling Process.

Counseling the High School Student Regarding Educational Plans.

Counseling the High School Student Regarding Vocational Plans.

Emphasis is placed in the first two sections upon use of guidance data in classroom situations. In Sections C, D and E techniques for using guidance data in individual counseling are outlined.

SECTION A. GUIDING STUDENTS REGARDING PHYSICAL AND MENTAL HEALTH.

Physiologists recognize a close relationship between mental and physical health. These two phases of growth and development are interdependent. Development of good physical health cannot be achieved unless there is also a satisfactory degree of mental health.

Educational personnel should be more aware of physical and mental health needs, growth and functions. An adequate guidance program will provide assistance to students in the development of satisfactory health understandings and habits, both physical and mental.

PART I. PHYSICAL HEALTH.

Physical Health Defined.

A health guidance program should help the student to attain a greater measure of physical well-being. This program consists of:

1. Helping students discover and correct inconsistencies in their health practices, attitudes and information.
2. Helping students discover and utilize their physical assets.

The Need for Health Guidance.

Recent medical findings provide evidence of the general need for health guidance on the high school level. In schools where authentic health practices, attitudes and information have been stressed, students have developed an active interest in their physical well-being.

Responsibility for Health Guidance.

Every classroom teacher should be constantly on the lookout for evidences among the students of deviations from normal health by observing such symptoms as:

1. Red eyes.
2. Coughing.
3. Mouth breathing.
4. Flushed face.

5. Pallor.
6. Fatigue.
7. Sleepiness.
8. Poor posture.
9. Excitability.
10. Overactiveness.
11. Skin eruption or sores.
12. Offensive breath, and the like.

When the teacher has observed symptoms such as those above, he should refer the student to a school nurse or physician for an examination. Health data gathered by physician, dentist, dental hygienist or nurse should be made available to the teacher or counselor. Caution must be exercised in permitting free access to confidential medical data. Some schools have found that a health committee composed of a cross-section of the faculty is helpful in determining policies for collecting and using health data.

Techniques for Dealing with Physical Health Problems

1. Collect information.

    This will include data on the following:

    a. Personal appearance.
    (1) Posture.
    (2) Skin.
    (3) Neuro-muscular responses.
    (4) Mannerisms.
    (5) Vitality.
    (6) Proper clothing.

    b. Growth and development pattern.
    (1) Body type.
    (2) Height.
    (3) Weight.
    (4) Proper nutrition.
    (5) Rate of gain (expected, actual, loss).

c. Defects and deviations from normal.

(1) Eyes.   (6) Teeth.
(2) Ears.   (7) Heart.
(3) Nose.   (8) Lungs.
(4) Throat.   (9) Coordination.
(5) Mouth.

d. Health practices and facts.

(1) Diet.   (5) Cleanliness.
(2) Sleep.   (6) Narcotics.
(3) Sex attitudes.   (7) Tobacco.
(4) Exercise.   (8) Alcohol.

2. Arrange school life to contribute to student's well-being.

a. School program.

(1) Student program load.
(2) Materials of instruction.
(3) Extracurricular activities.
(4) Teacher relationships.

b. Physical environment.

(1) Traffic hazards.
(2) Distance between home and school.
(3) School buildings and grounds.
    (a) Heat, light and ventilation.
    (b) Safety measures.
    (c) Provision for rest, relaxation and quiet.
    (d) Lunchroom and toilet facilities.

3. Assist parents to understand how home life may contribute to student's physical well-being.

a. Parental background and attitudes.

(1) Physical inheritance factors.
(2) Economic and educational status .
(3) Occupational classification.
(4) Health and emotional maturity.
(5) Attitudes toward school and social life.

b. Adequacy of home facilities.
  (1) Room and place for study.
  (2) Siblings.
  (3) Light, heat, ventilation.
  (4) Own room or bed.
4. Cooperate with community agencies in contributing to student's well-being.
  a. Physical environment.
    (1) Noise, odors, air pollution.
    (2) Food and water supply.
    (3) Accident hazards.
    (4) Sanitation.
  b. Socio-economic opportunities.
    (1) Wholesomeness of the community (moral standards).
    (2) Recreation (youth groups, playground facilities)
    (3) Religious environment.
    (4) Vocational opportunities.
    (5) Avocational (hobby) facilities.

Using Health Data in Physical Health Guidance.

Specific health needs among students may be found through the following devices:
1. Teacher and nurse observations.
2. Periodic health examinations.
3. Study of past health records.
4. Self-check charts.
5. Daily activity programs.
6. Physical performance tests.

After these data are obtained, they should be used to help the student determine:
1. The number of courses to be taken.
2. Type of physical education program.
3. Number of extracurricular activities.
4. Nutritional requirement (mid-morning lunch).

5. Special program adapted to individual needs.

6. General well-being.

The home, community and school environments should be carefully investigated. This may be accomplished by surveys planned by school personnel, or the school may use the surveys developed for this purpose by the Division of Health and Physical Education, Office of the Los Angeles County Superintendent of Schools.

The findings of the survey of the home and community environments may be presented to the school health education committee for consideration. Emphasis should be placed on the importance of attacking the problems most likely to yield immediate dividends.

Summary.

Guiding the high school student in health matters involves adequate information about his personal life, as well as his home, community and school life. Such data can be obtained by individual health examination, and through well-constructed questionnaires. It is recommended that the teacher and counselor should assist in health guidance as far as they are able. Some phases of health guidance, however, are highly specialized and need the services of physician or nurse. The person in charge of the program may find a health committee helpful in determining policies and procedures.

Suggested References.

Health Education. Report of Joint Committee on Health Problems in Education; Washington, D. C.: National Education Association, 1941.

Health in Schools. Twentieth Yearbook, American Association of School Administrators; Washington, D. C.: The Association, 1942.

Leonard, Margaret L., *Health Counseling for Girls.* New York: A. S. Barnes and Company, 1944.

Nash, J. B., *Teachable Moments.* New York: A. S. Barnes and Company, 1938.

Films on health subjects. (See publications of Division of Audio-Visual Education, Los Angeles County Superintendent of Schools.)

PART II. MENTAL HEALTH.

Mental Health Defined.

Guidance concerning mental health will assist the student to attain a greater measure of mental well-being. Mental health may be defined as the condition which enables an individual to adjust to the realities of life with a maximum of satisfaction to himself and to society.

Mental health may be improved by:

1. Prevention of the development of mental disorders.
2. Preservation of effective mental functioning.
3. Diagnosis and cure of mental illnesses after they have developed.

Guidance for mental health in the secondary school can contribute to the first two, and may contribute to number three by assisting the specialist to discover potential cases of mental illness.

Basic Principles of Mental Health.

1. Mental health is directly related to physical health.
2. Every individual should take a realistic attitude regarding his own qualifications and life in general.
3. Each individual needs to experience success as a means of gaining feelings of confidence and personal worth.
4. Controlled reactions to emotional situations are essential to maturity and stability.
5. Adjustment to conditions which cannot be changed is preferable to such reactions as worry, resentment and hatred.
6. A wholesome attitude toward sex is necessary.
7. Thoughtfulness and consideration of others are necessary in dealing effectively with people.
8. Balance between the extremes of independence-dependence, success-failure and relaxation-tension should be maintained in a constantly changing environment.

9. Participation in varied social activities is desirable.
10. Sympathetic understanding and an open mind are necessary to mental health.

Need for Mental Health Guidance.

Pre-war statistics indicate, and records of the armed services verify, the fact that an ever-increasing number of young people under the age of twenty-five are experiencing mental breakdowns. The alarming fact is that the number in this group is out of all proportion to the number of breakdowns in other age groups. Mental hygiene workers agree that neuroses and other maladjustments are as contagious as smallpox and diphtheria. There is an obvious need, therefore, for secondary schools to assume responsibility in helping adolescent youth to avoid mental illnesses.

Three approaches are feasible for the schools:

1. Helping students develop sound patterns of mental health.
2. Providing the classroom and school environment conducive to the preservation of effective mental functioning.
3. Offering a program of diagnosis and treatment suitable for maladjusted students.

Basic Human Needs.

Another evidence of the necessity for mental hygiene is found in the basic human needs inherent in all individuals as stated by Prescott. These are:

1. Physiological needs.
   a. air.
   b. food.
   c. water.
   d. shelter.
   e. activity and exercise.
   f. rest and relaxation.
   g. glandular balance.

2. Social or status needs.
   a. affection.
   b. belonging.
   c. personal worth.
   d. similarity to others.
3. Ego or integrative needs.
   a. adjustment to reality.
   b. ability to use words, numbers and other symbols.
   c. self-direction.
   d. a fair balance between success and failure.
   e. development of individuality.

Responsibility for Developing Better Mental Health Practices.

1. Teachers.

   Teachers should develop in their classrooms an emotional climate that is conducive to good mental health. In addition, the detection and prevention of maladjustment is a part of the classroom teacher's duties. When a case seems to be too involved for a teacher to secure adjustment through group techniques, the principal should request the assistance of a specialist such as a psychologist or the Research and Guidance Coordinator, who will then conduct an individual case study (see Chapter II, Section F).

   Teachers should be aware of the fact that the behavior difficulties of students are not mysterious maladies but are the logical outcomes of certain specific experiences in their lives as small children. Teachers need to understand that **symptoms are not true causes, but evidences of underlying causes,** which need detailed study. There is a cause for every symptom but it probably will not be found on the surface. Very often these causes are found to lie right in the school itself and in the classroom; in the very attitude of the teacher and the **emotional climate of the schoolroom.**

Examples of Classroom Emotional Climate.

a. If Miss Smith knows that Judy is a shy, backward, unwanted girl in a broken family where she experiences no love or affection, she will, if she is a good teacher, show Judy that she is well liked by the teacher, and attempt to arrange little situations whereby Judy can be encouraged and can capitalize on certain of her specific assets and thereby gain attention and status from her classmates. School can be made to supplement and implement an ineffectual home situation, so Judy will have the experience of feeling **needed** and **important** in her school group, even though she is ignored or criticized at home.

b. In contrast to Miss Smith's technique, Miss Jones demands instant obedience, utter silence and military-like precision from all her students; she insists to the superintendent that Tom is a ruffian and will come to no good end, and therefore she will "wash her hands" of him. She is instantly and highly shocked at Bill's frank references to sex, and feels that he is hopelessly bad. Is it any wonder, then, that Miss Jones seems to have more than her average share of problem students? Has Miss Jones ever consciously stopped to consider that possibly her students may have a problem teacher? A change of attitude, alone, will create certain improvements in the emotional climate of Miss Jones' classroom. Other changes will require definite study and effort, and will need much understanding and kindness on her part, rather than criticism and ridicule of her students.

c. Joe, sixteen years of age, under-developed, timid, nervous and apprehensive, was a potential stutterer. He had a protruding set of teeth, his hair was wiry and unruly. His eyes were small and almost buried under heavy eyebrows. In addition, he was forced to wear shabby clothes because of the poor economic condition of his family. He also had to bear the nagging of a critical stepfather.

Joe had never been able to speak very well but slipped by because he had always attended the same school. However, when in the 9th grade, he was forced to move to a strange school. Entering a new class, he was required to stand before the group, give his name and tell where he came from. Embarrassed and frightened, he spoke in an almost inaudible voice. The teacher snapped sharply, "Speak up, you sound as if your mouth were full of mush!" Joe began to stutter and the teacher said, "Oh! You're a stutterer—no wonder you can't talk!" Now, Joe bears a label, and he is set aside from other students as "a stutterer"!

Joe's stuttering developed because he was humiliated and frightened before a strange group. Had the teacher greeted Joe in a friendly manner, secured his name quietly and made him feel at home, he probably would have adjusted satisfactorily to the new environment. Rejection at school, added to home criticism and inadequacy was too much. His maladjustment became apparent in stuttering. Now, Joe's problem is a difficult one because he is labeled. He will need the help of a sympathetic and understanding specialist.

2. Administrators and Supervisors.

The administrator is responsible for organizing and supporting a secondary school program that will provide for the mental hygiene needs of both students and teachers. A flexible and functional curriculum should be provided to meet the individual needs, capacities and interests of the full range of students. To do this adequately, the administrator and supervising personnel will, themselves, need to be relatively free from personality maladjustments.

Techniques for Dealing with Mental Health Problems.

1. Collect information.

   Techniques for collecting and organizing information about students are outlined in Chapter II. These include the testing program, cumulative records, observation, anecdotal records, autobiography, interview, questionnaire and case study.

2. Identify obvious symptoms of mental maladjustment such as:[1]

   a. Childishness, sulking, crying, pouting, hitting, temper tantrums, pretending to be ill.

   b. Sensitiveness, self-concern, daydreaming, tending to alibi.

   c. Inferiority, incompetency, self-debasement, fearfulness.

   d. Self-consciousness concerning physical defects or personal appearance.

   e. Persistent nervous mannerisms, nail-biting, facial twitching, stuttering and the like.

3. Recognize that good mental health requires the development of certain qualities, characteristics and concepts, such as:

   a. Friendliness, sense of security and well-being.

---

[1]Thorpe, Louis P., and Clark, Willis W., *Manual of Directions, Mental Health Analysis*, Secondary Series (Los Angeles: California Test Bureau, 1946).

     b. Social competence, concern for others, subordination of selfish motives.

4. Encourage the teacher to consider his own mental health and its effect upon the class. The main prerequisite to school-wide mental health is that all school personnel themselves be relatively free from maladjustments.

5. Make possible social adjustment through the educational program. (Refer to Chapter IV and Chapter V, Section B.)

6. Arrange the physical equipment of the classroom informally.

7. Employ democratic procedure in the classroom and develop wise use of student leadership.

8. Make effective use of leisure time and extracurricular activities.

9. Arrange for individual case studies where needed.

    The teacher should refer to the administrator, students who need further individual study by the Coordinator of Research and Guidance. (See Chapter II, Section F.)

Summary.

Mental health is the condition which enables an individual to adjust to the realities of life with a maximum of satisfaction to himself and to society.

Three aspects of mental health are: prevention of mental disorders, maintenance of sound mental functioning and diagnosis and cure of mental illnesses.

Inherent in all individuals are certain basic human needs which require the application of mental health principles: physiological, social, personal and psychological. Teachers, adminstrators and specialists have a responsibility for the utilization of specific techniques conducive to good mental health.

The main prerequisite to school-wide mental health is that all school personnel, themselves, be relatively free from maladjustments.

Suggested References.

Cobb, Stanley, *Borderland of Psychiatry*. Cambridge, Massachusetts: Harvard University Press, 1943.

Crow, Lester D., and Crow, Alice, *Mental Hygiene in School and Home Life*. New York: McGraw-Hill Book Company, 1942.

Fenton, Norman, *Mental Hygiene in School Practice*. Palo Alto, California: Stanford University Press, 1943.

Prescott, Daniel A., *Emotion and the Educative Process*. Washington, D. C.: American Council on Education, 1938.

Thorpe, Louis P., *Child Psychology and Development*. New York: The Ronald Press Company, 1946.

_____*Psychological Foundations of Personality*. New York: McGraw-Hill Book Company, 1938.

_____and Clark, Willis W., *Manual of Directions, Mental Health Analysis*, Secondary Series. Los Angeles: California Test Bureau, 1946.

Tiegs, E. W., and Katz, Barney, *Mental Hygiene in Education*. New York: The Ronald Press Company, 1941.

SECTION B.   GUIDING STUDENTS REGARDING PERSONAL-SOCIAL PROBLEMS.

The attainment of adulthood is a difficult and complex process. Many parents and teachers, however, have assumed that a natural complement of the physical growth of students is the development of social and emotional maturity. It is now known that such an assumption is not in line with the facts. Psychologists have discovered that specific help must be provided in many cases if the student is to achieve social and emotional maturity.

Development of the capacity for maintaining personal status, without alienating the respect and acceptance of others, is so complex that most individuals do not achieve this maturity without definite help. This help was provided formerly by the home. Many American homes are now unable or unwilling to provide this kind of direction. Thus the school must assume greater responsibility for personal-social guidance.

Meaning of the Term Personal-Social Guidance.

Personal-social guidance assists the student to achieve freedom from inner conflict and to make satisfying adaptations to his environment. Such guidance also involves preventive and corrective approaches to the conditions confronted by students as social individuals.

Personal-Social Problems of High School Students.

Among the problems confronted by high school students are:

1. Emotional Problems.

   Observation leads to the conclusion that many student responses are influenced by emotional urges more often than by objective reasoning and judgment. This need not be the case if the student can secure personal-social guidance that will contribute to his growth of emotional control. Development of such control will give richness and fullness to life. Students should be guided in the following:

   a. Cultivation of emotional balance.

   b. Development of a sense of belonging.

   c. Acceptance of success with humility.

   d. Achievement of capacity for proper self-evaluation.

    e. Protection of the rights of others in exercising individual freedom of choice.

    f. Attainment of individual characteristics that will prepare for worthy home membership.

2. Social Problems.

    a. Making friends.

    b. Developing courtesy.

    c. Practicing social etiquette.

    d. Understanding socially acceptable practices.

    e. Building social poise.

    f. Learning to participate in social activities, such as:

        (1) Dancing.

        (2) Sports.

        (3) Games.

        (4) Clubs.

        (5) Parties and the like.

    g. Problems of Boy-Girl Relations.

        (1) Physical development (See Chapter I).

        (2) Emotional development.

        (3) Social customs.

           (a) Making dates.

           (b) Going steady.

           (c) Solving problems of dress.

        (4) Congenial relationships.

           (a) Courtesies.

           (b) Varied social activities.

           (c) Group activities versus cliques.

           (d) Problems of expenses.

    h. Problem of Smoking.

        (1) Social implications—rights of others.

        (2) Personal implications—physical, mental and emotional.

    i. Problem of Drinking.

       (1) Social implications—effect on others.

       (2) Personal implications—physical, moral and emotional.

    j. The Automobile Problem.

       (1) Safe driving and highway courtesy.

       (2) Car ownership and use.

    k. Problem of Wise Use of Leisure Time.

3. Economic Problems.

    a. Securing and holding a position (See Chapter V, Section E, on Vocational Problems).

    b. Satisfying needs for:

       (1) Food.

       (2) Clothing.

       (3) Living quarters.

       (4) Recreation, transportation, communication and the like.

    c. Thrift and budgeting.

4. Personal Problems.

    a. Understanding one's physical development.

       (1) Problems of sex.

       (2) Problems of adolescent growth.

    b. Establishing adequate physical, mental and emotional habits.

    c. Preparing for marriage.

       (1) Mature love versus emotion.

       (2) Unselfishness versus selfishness.

       (3) Marriage versus a career.

       (4) Understanding the problem of sex.

       (5) Petting.

(6) Early marriage versus long engagement.

(7) The money problem.

   (a) Shall wife work?

   (b) Who shall control finances?

(8) Building for compatibility.

   (a) Courtesy.

   (b) Respect for rights of partner.

   (c) Character and self-control.

   (d) Loyalty to family.

   (e) Emotional stability.

d. Building desirable patterns for living.

(1) Self-realization.

(2) Human relationships.

(3) Economic efficiency.

(4) Civic responsibilty.

Procedures for Helping Students Solve Personal-Social Problems.

1. Determining the personal-social needs of high school students.

   a. Observation and anecdotal records (See Chapter II).

   By raising a few questions, the teacher can learn a great deal about the personal-social needs of students.

   Does the Student:

   (1) Seem to have close friends?

   (2) Appear at ease in a group?

   (3) Become emotional in discussing controversial problems?

   (4) Participate in group activity?

   (5) Appear to be moody?

(6) Possess persistent nervous mannerisms, such as finger tapping, nail biting, excessive blinking of eyes, head jerking, lip biting, cracking of finger joints and the like?

(7) Seem insecure, aggressive or over-active?

(8) Seem willing to accept responsibility?

(9) Possess speech difficulties, such as lisping, stuttering, jerky enunciation or high-pitched voice?

(10) Appear overly-conscious of personal appearance?

b. Inventories of personal-social adjustment may offer assistance to the teacher in determining personal-social needs of students. Does the student:

(1) Show self-reliance?

(2) Have a feeling of belonging?

(3) Possess social skills?

(4) Enjoy good school relations?

2. Providing for personal-social needs of high school students.

a. Group Techniques.

(1) Arrange the work of each class to meet the personal-social needs of individual students.

(2) Correlate the work of other classes in relation to information on personal-social needs.

(3) Stimulate student participation by means of student body and extracurricular activities.

(4) Stimulate students to identify personal-social problems with which school personnel may be of assistance.

(5) Secure help of class in arranging situations which may encourage timid and emotional students to participate.

b. Individual Techniques, (Consult Section C of this Chapter and Section F of Chapter II).

c. Following is a list of books which offer personal-social guidance to students:

Bennett, Margaret E., and Hand, Harold C., *Beyond High School.* Group Guidance Series, Volume III; New York: McGraw-Hill Book Company, 1938.

_____, *Design for Personality.* Group Guidance Series, Volume II; New York: McGraw-Hill Book Company, 1938.

_____, *School and Life.* Group Guidance Series, Volume I; New York: McGraw-Hill Book Company, 1938.

Brainard, Paul, *What About Yourself?* Los Angeles: H. H. McClure Publishing Company, 1939.

Brown, Howard E., *Your Life in a Democracy.* Chicago: J. B. Lippincott Company, 1944.

Clark, Edwin L., *Petting—Wise or Otherwise.* New York: Association Press, 1939.

Crawford, C. C., et al., *Living Your Life.* New York: D. C. Heath and Company, 1940.

Eichler, Lillian, *The New Etiquette.* New York: Garden City Publishing Company, 1939.

Folsom, Joseph K., *Plan for Marriage.* New York: Harper and Brothers, 1938.

Goodrich, Laurence B., *Living with Others.* San Francisco: American Book Company, 1939.

Head, Gay, *Boy Dates Girl.* New York: Scholastic Corporation, 1937.

Landis, Paul H., and Landis, Judson T., *Social Living.* San Francisco: Ginn and Company, 1938.

Uhl, Willis L., and Powers, Francis E., *Personal and Social Adjustment.* New York: The Macmillan Company, 1938.

Films on personal-social problems. (See publications of Division of Audio-Visual Education, Los Angeles County Superintendent of Schools.)

"Junior Prom"—Produced by Semmel Merseroey.

"Family Teamwork"—Emily Frith.

Summary.

Many students are not receiving satisfactory home assistance in relation to personal-social problems. Aid in developing the ability and skill to meet emotional, social, economic and personal problems is one of the most important services that the secondary school can render to students. It is in this personal-social problem area that guidance renders a valuable service.

Suggested References (for Teachers).

Chisolm, Leslie L., *Guiding Youth in the Secondary School.* San Francisco: American Book Company, 1945.

Crow, Lester D., and Crow, Alice, *Mental Hygiene in School and Home Life.* New York: McGraw-Hill Book Company, 1942.

Dunbar, H. Flanders, new edition, *Emotions and Bodily Changes.* New York: Columbia University Press, 1939.

Goldstein, Sydney E., *Marriage and Family Counseling.* New York: McGraw-Hill Book Company, 1941.

Lloyd-Jones, Esther and Fedder, Ruth, *Coming of Age.* New York: McGraw-Hill Book Company, 1941.

Murray, Elwood, *The Speech Personality.* Chicago: J. B. Lippincott Company, 1946.

Tryon, Caroline McCann, *Evaluation of Adolescent Personality by Adolescents.* Society for Research in Child Development; Washington, D. C.: National Research Council, 1940.

Tyler, Harry E., and Others, *Learning to Live.* New York: Farrar and Rinehart, 1940.

SECTION C. THE COUNSELING PROCESS.

What is the Counseling Process?

The counseling process involves one or more interactions between the student and the counselor for the purpose of assisting the student to make satisfying adjustments to his problems. These adjustments may be made after an adequate appraisal of the student's aptitudes, capacities, interests, aspirations and opportunities. Often this will lead to a suitable, long-range plan instead of a choice based upon expediency.

The counseling process is directly related to the interview; in fact, the interview has been described as the heart of the counseling proceess. Suggested procedures for using the interview as a means of gathering student data were discussed in detail in Section B of Chapter II. These same techniques apply during the counseling process in giving information and assisting in making adjustments.

The chief value of the counseling process is to assist the student to understand his problems and possible solutions. Frequently a therapeutic value is derived in addition to diagnosis.

During the counseling process, it is necessary to consider the needs of the total student rather than to isolate any specific items of his environment or of himself.

The objectives of the counseling process are to assist the student to:

1. Appraise his assets and liabilities.
2. Understand demands and benefits of the specific situations.
3. Plan a program of action.
4. Put the plan into effect.
5. Make adjustments to changing conditions.

The Need for Counseling.

Since adjustments will be made on an individual basis, the counseling services must be available for all students. In many cases information and tests may be accomplished on a group basis, but it is also necessary to realize that each individual has needs and problems unique to himself. The counseling process will help the students to know themselves as individuals and as members of society. It will also help them to correct shortcomings, to take advantage of special abilities, to compensate for handicaps and to expand interests.

Who Usually Does the Counseling?

The counseling process will not be the responsibility of any one individual, but rather the combined responsibility of the student, the counselor, the teachers, the specialists and the administrators. The counselor who has been specially trained in the problems of adolescence should be responsible for the basic planning of the counseling program. Each teacher should be responsible for such counseling as the individual student ordinarily may need. In many cases the student should be referred to a specialist for specific information or special tests. In some cases, the student will have to do much of the work himself under supervision so that he will appreciate the value of the information. The student must make his own decision, after all the facts have been carefully considered.

Suggestions for Counseling Students.

1. Gather useful personal data.

    In order to cultivate self-understanding, certain information must be collected and studied. The technique for collecting this student information is discussed in detail in the various sections of Chapter II. Some more important items are:

    a. Home and family background.

    b. School history and record of class work.

    c. Test results—mental maturity, achievement and others.

    d. Physical health and physique.

    e. Mental health.

    f. Work experience.

    g. Leisure time activities.

    h. Social experiences.

    i. Educational capacity.

    j. Vocational interests.

    k. Aptitudes and talents.

2. Analyze types of problems.

High school students have many problems. The following are typical problem areas:

    a. Educational planning.

    b. Educational adjustment.

    c. Physical health.

    d. Mental health.

    e. Vocational planning.

    f. Leisure time.

    g. Personal-social.

    h. Financial.

    i. Marriage and family.

    j. Civic responsibility.

For many students it would be difficult to isolate only one problem in the above areas. The counselor should be alert to the many factors underlying the student's difficulties.

In some cases, persons other than the student and the counselor will be involved. Often parents can be brought in to provide further background information. They can also assume their portion of the responsibility in helping the student to develop and carry through his plan of action. In some types of problems, other persons will be in a position to provide information, particularly in subject-matter and interest areas.

3. Investigate sources of information.

Sometimes it will be necessary to have additional information from outside sources to assist the student in his solution. For special references see Chapter IV.

4. Select appropriate techniques.

The counseling process has three purposes: (a) get information; (b) give information and (c) improve adjustment. Many approaches may be used in counseling; however, there are two well-defined procedures, usually called the "direct" and the "indirect." The most effective use of these techniques is presented in the references at the end of this chapter. The specific technique or combination used by the counselor should depend upon the interpretation of the needs of the student.

5. Follow recommended interviewing procedures.

Since the interview is the essential part of counseling, a review of the important steps is presented:

a. Prepare adequately for the interview.

b. Establish friendly relationship.

c. Use suitable techniques.

d. Terminate the interview appropriately.

e. Record significant results of interview.

Counseling may include combinations of both formal and informal interviews and should be recognized as a continuing process.

6. Making and carrying through plans of action.

One desirable outcome of the counseling process is the formulation of a plan of action. The counselor is responsible for helping the student consider all phases of the problem in formulating such a plan. The final decision, however, with respect to the value of each part of the plan is the responsibility of the student. In carrying through, both counselor and student should be ready to alter the plan as changing conditions require.

Summary.

The counseling process involves one or more interactions between student and counselor for the purpose of assisting a student to make satisfying adjustments. Through counseling, the student should be able better to appraise himself and his situation, to plan a program of action and to follow the plan successfully. All students need counseling service. Both school personnel and students must cooperate to make counseling most successful.

Suggested References.

Darley, John, Testing and Counseling in the High School Guidance Program. Chicago: Science Research Associates, 1943.

Paterson, D. G., et al., Student Guidance Techniques. New York: McGraw-Hill Book Company, 1938.

Rogers, Carl R., Counseling and Psychotherapy. Boston: Houghton-Mifflin Company, 1942.

_____"Significant Aspects of Client-Centered Therapy," The American Psychologist, 1:10, October, 1946.

Rogers, C. R., and Wallen, J. L., Counseling With Returned Servicemen. New York: McGraw-Hill Book Company, 1946.

Thorne, F. C., "A Critique of Nondirective Methods of Psychotherapy," Journal of Abnormal and Social Psychology, 39, 459-470, 1944.

_____"Directive Psychotherapy," Journal of Clinical Psychology, 2: 68-79, 1946.

Williamson, E. G., How to Counsel Students. New York: McGraw-Hill Book Company, 1939.

Williamson, E. G., and Darley, J. E., Student Personnel Work. New York: McGraw-Hill Book Company, 1937.

Williamson, E. G., and Hahn, M. E., Introduction to High School Counseling. New York: McGraw-Hill Book Company, 1940.

SECTION D. COUNSELING THE HIGH SCHOOL STUDENT REGARDING EDUCATIONAL PLANS.

Educational Guidance.

Educational guidance is a process of assisting the individual to plan, carry through and make adjustments in his educational program in the light of his interests, capacities and needs. Educational guidance is chiefly concerned with school orientation, student programming with choice of electives, graduation requirements, college-entrance requirements, further educational opportunities, better study habits and miscellaneous educational information. Counseling the student concerning educational choices must be based upon individual needs and abilities. (See Chapter I, Section C for differing characteristics of students.)

The Role of Educational Guidance.

High school students need educational guidance to enable them to get maximum profit from high school offerings, to plan for the successful completion of high school, and to choose post high school instructional opportunities. Such basic educational needs as the following should be kept in mind by the counselor:

1. Perspective of student's complete high school program.
2. Fulfillment of high school requirements.
3. Choice of electives upon the basis of genuine interests, needs and abilities.
4. Selection of appropriate extracurricular activities.
5. Understanding of the guidance value of specific courses.
6. Adjustment of program to meet changing conditions.
7. Selection of post high school training institution.

8. Choice of post high school course or curriculum.

9. Fulfillment of enrollment requirements for post high school training institution.

Responsibility for Educational Guidance.

Educational guidance is the joint responsibility of the faculty, students and parents. In addition, selected specialists may be called upon for educational counseling concerning preparation for specific occupations. Faculty, students, parents and specialists have the following responsibilities:

1. The administrator has the responsibility of arranging an adequate school schedule to facilitate educational guidance.

2. Counselors should appraise student assets, outline educational opportunities and help the student match his individual abilities with the most appropriate learning activities.

3. The teacher should offer educational information to the student, help him better to understand himself and continuously assist him in improving his study habits.

4. Parents should cooperate with the school personnel in planning the educational program best suited to the student's ability, occupational choice and further training prospects.

5. Specialists may be selected to advise concerning the amount and most appropriate type of training required for certain vocations and chosen fields of activities.

6. Students should cooperate with the school personnel and parents in the process of planning, adjusting and carrying through their educational programs.

How to Make Educational Guidance Effective.

Many methods are being used to make educational guidance effective. The following are samples of representative practices pertaining to:

1. School orientation.

     School orientation is a means of acquainting the student with educational requirements and opportunities. The following sources are helpful:

     a. Handbooks and bulletins.

     b. School paper.

     c. Assembly programs for new students.

     d. Guidance classes (See Chapter V).

     e. Interviews with counselor or guidance teacher.

2. Student programming with choice of electives.

     Student programming requires first a choice between college and non-college attendance. The counselor offering educational guidance should study the cumulative record of the student carefully to help him select a college or non-college program. Following are examples of curricula which may be recommended:

     a. College program (for 10th grade).

     English ....10 semester hours (1 credit)

     Physical Education 10

     Geometry 10

     Foreign Language...............10

     Elective (Art, Biology, History, Home Economics, Music, Industrial Arts,

     Typing) 10

b. Non-college program (for 10th grade).

The non-college program may be scheduled in one of several interest fields: agriculture, art, commercial, home economics, industrial arts, music and others.

Following is an example of a non-college 10th grade music program:

English ....10 semester hours (1 credit)

Physical Education 10

Major Subject (any
    music course) 10

Biology 10
French, German, History
    or other Elective...............10

In programming the student, some schools prefer to have the student plan his complete high school schedule in the freshman year as a means of giving him adequate perspective and direction. At the time of programming, the values and characteristics of both required and elective subjects should be explained to the student. Following is an example of the way in which some courses may be related to occupations:

Subject	Related Occupational Fields
Agriculture	Agricultural engineering; agriculture education; agronomy and soil science; animal and poultry husbandry; dairy science; entomology; forestry; horticulture; plant pathology; teaching.
English	English courses are essential for all careers. Basic for architecture, engineering, journalism, law, medicine, teaching, writing and others.

Geography	Agricultural science; anthropology; economics; geology; history; international relations; political science; public health; teaching.
Journalism	Advertising agencies; free-lance writing; press services; proof reading; public relations; radio; syndicates; teaching.
Mathematics	Astronomy; chemistry; engineering; insurance field (actuarial work); meteorology; physics; statistics; teaching.
Music	Composition; music critic; music librarian; music publishing; music store work; player or director; radio; movies; opera; recreation; teaching; writing and editing.
Physical Education	Coaching; personnel; physical therapy; public health; recreation; safety; social work.

c. School-parent cooperation in programming.

Faculty, parents and students should cooperate in planning a program to fulfill requirements and to choose electives consistent with individual student assets. Following is a form which has been used by one school as a worksheet for student programming:

9th GRADE PROGRAM PLAN

Last Name .... First Name .... Grade .... Room .... Date ....

PRESENT PROGRAM   Grade

NEXT SEMESTER'S PLAN   Grade

1-2. Social Living ....

3. Science or Algebra ....
   (cross out the one not taken)

4. Physical Ed. ....

5. ....

6. ....

Alternate Electives
   (in case of conflict)

1. ....

2. ....

3. ....

Electives approved:

....
Signature of student

....
Signature of parent or guardian

....
Signature of guidance teacher

PRESENT PROGRAM   Grade

1-2. Social Living ....

3. Physical Ed. ....

4. ....

5. ....

6. ....

Did you take typing in A8
semester? ....

Did you take Foreign Language
in the A8 semester? ....
If so, which one? ....

Did you take shop in the
A8 semester? ....

Have you planned your life
work yet? ....
If so, what is it to be? ....

Do you plan to finish high
school? ....
College? ....

DUPLICATE PLAN
To be retained by Guidance Teacher

Name .... Room .... Date ....

NEXT SEMESTER'S PLAN   Grade

1-2. Social Living ....

3. Science or Algebra ....
   (cross out the one not taken)

4. Physical Ed. ....

5. ....

6. ....

Alternate Electives
   (in case of conflict)

1. ....

2. ....

3. ....

Electives approved:

....
Signature of student

....
Signature of parent or guardian

....
Signature of guidance teacher

3. Graduation requirements.

The student should be informed concerning all graduation requirements at the time of programming. The counselor should check to make sure that all requirements of the curriculum chosen have been included in the total program. Following is a list of both general and departmental requirements for graduation as outlined by one senior high school:

a. General requirements.

B-10	A-10	B-11
Phys. Ed. B-10 Eng. Life Sci. I or B-10 Soc. St. *Pract. Art Major Subj.	Phys. Ed. A-10 Eng. A-10 Soc. St. or Life Sc. I *Art Major Subj.	Phys. Ed. B-11 Eng. B-11 Soc. St. **Lab. Sci. I *Music Major Subj.

A-11	B-12	A-12
Phys. Ed. A-11 Eng. or **Eng. elect. A-11 Soc. St. **Lab. Sci. II Major Subj.	Phys. Ed. Major Subj.	Phys. Ed. Sr. Prob. Major Subj.

PLUS: electives or major requirements to total a minimum of 20 units per semester, not including Phys. Ed.

*May be taken any semester.

**May be taken any time in grades 11 or 12.

b. Departmental requirements (in addition to general requirements).

Bookkeeping Major (example).

4 semesters Bookkeeping.

2 semesters Typing.

2 semesters Business Practice.

1 semester Business Law.

1 semester Business Correspondence.*

*Business correspondence may count for English in Bookkeeping major.

4. College entrance requirements.

In addition to graduation requirements, college entrance requirements must be checked for college preparatory students. Enrollment requirements differ greatly from college to college, and change occasionally. Counselors should give accurate and up-to-date information concerning college entrance requirements when programming the student. This information may be secured from college bulletins and condensed in usable tabular form. Following is a condensed list of requirements for one college:

6 semesters English   2 semesters Algebra
2 semesters U. S. History and Civics   2 semesters Geometry
     2 semesters Language
2 semesters Science
     Special Requirement (Special Requirement may be 3rd year of Math; or Chemistry or Physics or 3rd year of a language, or two years of a second language).

To make sure that both graduation and college enrollment requirements have been fulfilled, the student's program should be listed by subjects on one sheet. This check should be made at the beginning of each of the high school years so that incompletes and failures may be brought up to date.

The following form has been devised by a senior high school counselor:

REQUIREMENTS WORK SHEET
Senior High School

--------------------------------   --------------------------------

Student's Last Name   First Name   Date Expects to Graduate

Student's Destination: College......Non-College......Occupation....

	Completed	Taking	To Take	Remarks
Graduation requirements.........				
English (20 sem. hrs.).............				
Major (30).............................				
Social Studies (11th yr.) (10) (Incl. U.S. History and Civics)...				
Laboratory Science (10)............				
Physical Education (30)............				
Art.................................				
Music................................				
Practical Arts (5)...................				
Senior Problems (5).................				
Total—150 Semester Hrs...........				
College Entrance Requirements				
English (6)..........................				
Social Studies (2)...................				
Science (2)...........................				
Algebra (2) & Geometry (2).....				
Language (4).........................				
Requirements (F) (2)...............				

COURSES TO BE COMPLETED

10th Grade Program	11th Grade Program	12th Grade Program
Physical Education	Physical Education	Physical Education

Signed........................   Signed........................   Signed........................
Student   Student   Student

Signed........................   Signed........................   Signed........................
Counselor   Counselor   Counselor

5. Further Educational Opportunities.

Students in the college group need counseling concerning the choice of the most appropriate college in line with their assets and vocational plans. Students in the non-college group need even more counseling concerning post high school training opportunities. These opportunities include junior colleges, adult schools, trade schools, extension and correspondence courses, a long list of private schools and private study through books and libraries. For an extended list of trade, commercial and miscellaneous schools, consult the **List of California Educational Institutions Approved to Offer Training to Veterans,** California State Department of Education, Sacramento, California, September, 1946. Following is a list of public and semi-public schools frequently entered by students from Los Angeles County:

Colleges and Universities: (Public)
 Chico State College, Chico.
 Fresno State College, Fresno.
 Humboldt State College, Arcata.
 Los Angeles State College, Los Angeles.
 San Diego State College, San Diego.
 San Francisco State College, San Francisco.
 San Jose State College, San Jose.
 University of California:
  Berkeley Campus.
  Los Angeles Campus.
  Santa Barbara Campus.
  Davis Campus.
  San Francisco Campus.

Colleges and Universities: (Private)
 California College of Arts and Crafts, Broadway and
  College Avenue, Oakland.
 California Institute of Technology, Pasadena.
 Chapman College, 766 North Vermont Avenue, Los
  Angeles.
 Claremont Graduate School, Claremont.
 College of the Pacific, Stockton.

Heald Engineering College, Van Ness Avenue at Post Street, San Francisco.

La Verne College, La Verne.

Lincoln University, 1101 Masonic Ave., San Francisco.

Los Angeles Pacific College, 5732 Ebey Avenue, Los Angeles.

Loyola University of Los Angeles, 7101 W. 80th St., Los Angeles.

Mills College, Oakland.

Occidental College, 1600 Campus Road, Los Angeles.

Pasadena College, 1539 E. Howard St., Pasadena.

Pepperdine College, 1121 W. 79th St., Los Angeles.

Pomona College, Claremont.

St. Mary's College, St. Mary's College.

Santa Clara University, Santa Clara.

Scripps College, Claremont.

Stanford University, Stanford University.

University of Redlands, Redlands.

University of San Francisco, San Francisco.

University of Southern California, Los Angeles

Whittier College, Whittier.

Evening Adult Schools in Los Angeles County:

Alhambra City Evening High School, 308 West Main St., Alhambra.

Beverly Hills Evening High School, 241 Moreno Dr., Beverly Hills.

Bonita Union Evening High School, Bonita Avenue, La Verne.

Burbank Evening High School, 902 North Third St., Burbank.

Centinela Valley Adult Education Division, 235 South Grevillea, Inglewood.

Citrus Union High School (Junior College and Evening High School), 1436 East Foothill Blvd., Azusa.

Compton Evening Junior College, 601 South Acacia St., Compton.

Downey Evening High School, 319 East Firestone Blvd., Downey.

El Monte Evening High School, 712 South Tyler Ave., El Monte.

Excelsior Evening High School, Corner Pioneer and Center, Norwalk.

Glendale Evening High School, 1440 East Broadway, Glendale.

Glendale Evening Junior College, 1500 North Verdugo Rd., Glendale.

Herbert Hoover Evening High School, 651 Glenwood Road, Glendale.

Los Angeles City Evening High Schools:

Banning, Phineas, 1500 Avalon Blvd., Wilmington.
Bell-South Gate, 4328 Bell Ave., Bell.
Belmont, 1575 West Second St., L. A.
Fairfax, 7850 Melrose Ave., L. A.
Francis, John H., Polytechnic.
Franklin, Benjamin, 820 No. Avenue 54.
Fremont, John C., 7676 South San Pedro St.
Hollywood High School, 1521 North Highland Ave.
Huntington Park High School, 6020 Miles Avenue, Huntington Park.
Jefferson, Thomas, 1319 East 41st Street.
Lincoln, Abraham, 3501 North Broadway.
Los Angeles High School, 4600 Olympic Blvd.
Manual Arts High School, 4131 South Vermont Ave.
Metropolitan High School, 234 Venice Blvd.
North Hollywood High School, 5231 Colfax Avenue, North Hollywood.
Roosevelt, Theodore, 4500 South Fickett Street.
San Pedro High School, 1001 W. 15th St., San Pedro.
University High School, 11800 Texas Avenue.
Van Nuys High School, 6535 Cedros Avenue, Van Nuys.
Venice High School, 13000 Venice Blvd., Venice.
Washington, George, 10860 Denker Avenue.
Wiggins, Frank, Trade High School, 1646 So. Olive.

Monrovia-Arcadia-Duarte Evening High School, Colorado and Madison, Monrovia.

Montebello Evening High School, 1600 Whittier Blvd., Montebello.

Pomona City High School Division of Adult Education (Evening School), Holt and San Antonio Avenues, Pomona.

Redondo Evening High School, Corner Diamond and Elena Sts., Redondo Beach.

Santa Monica Adult Education Center, 7th St. and Michigan Ave., Santa Monica.

South Pasadena-San Marino Evening High School, 1327 Diamond Avenue, South Pasadena.

Whittier School of Adult Education (Evening School), 610 West Philadelphia Street, Whittier.

Junior Colleges in Los Angeles County:

Antelope Valley Union High School (Junior College), Lancaster.

Compton Junior College, 601 So. Acacia St., Compton.

El Camino Junior College, P. O. Box 28, Inglewood.

Glendale Junior College, 1500 North Verdugo Road, Glendale.

Long Beach City College:

Liberal Arts Division, 4901 East Carson Blvd., Long Beach.

East Long Beach Adult Center, 7th Street and Euclid Ave., Long Beach.

North Long Beach Adult Center, 4901 East Carson Blvd., Long Beach.

Polytechnic Adult Center, Rm. 401, 16th St. and Atlantic Ave., Long Beach.

Technical Institute Division, 8th St. and Locust Ave., Long Beach.

Los Angeles City College, 855 North Vermont Ave., Los Angeles.

East Los Angeles Junior College, 5027 East Sixth St., Los Angeles.

Mt. San Antonio Junior College, P.O. Box 801, Pomona.

Pasadena Junior College, 1570 East Colorado St., Pasadena.

Santa Monica City College, 7th St. and Michigan Ave., Santa Monica.

Trade and Miscellaneous Schools:

California Maritime Academy, 515 Van Ness Avenue, San Francisco.

California Polytechnic School, San Luis Obispo.

Long Beach Technical Institute, 8th and Locust Ave., Long Beach.

Santa Monica Technical High School (Evening), 22nd
St. and Virginia, Santa Monica.
Wiggins, Frank, Trade High School, 1646 So. Olive,
Los Angeles.

6. Better Study Habits.

All students can profit by some educational counseling concerning the improvement of their study habits.
A few are destined to failure in high school unless considerable help in how to study is given.

Even though no two students ever need the same
counseling in how to study, the following general suggestions may be adapted to individual needs:

a. Work out with the student a plan for budgeting and
spacing work, rest and recreation.

b. Encourage the student and his parents to provide
a comfortable, quiet, healthful room in which to do
homework.

c. Suggest ways of protecting health and vitality.

d. Explain the necessity for sufficient interest and motivation.

e. Help outline a long-range study plan.

f. Show student how to understand better the purposes
for studying a given unit or subject.

g. Tell the student how to build habits of concentration and memorization of vital points.

h. Demonstrate to the student an effective system of
note taking and filing.

i. Stress outlining, note taking and filing.

j. Offer directions in the use of sources such as dic-
tionaries, indexes, appendixes, glossaries, libraries
and depositaries.

k. Stress continued improvement in writing, reading,
vocabulary and interpretation.

    l. Encourage careful selection of books, lectures and conferences.

    m. Point out the importance of systematic review and evalution.

    n. Provide situations for practicing or using what has been learned.

7. Miscellaneous Educational Information.

Students need educational counseling with respect to additional aspects of their school experiences. They need both information and help in making proper interpretations regarding the following items:

    a. Fees, tuitions and other school expenses.

    b. Opportunities for part-time work.

    c. Fellowships and scholarships.

    d. Loan funds.

    e. Educational values in extracurricular activities.

    f. Cost of room and board.

    g. Educational services by other community agencies.

    h. Recreational facilities connected with school.

    i. Definition of terms such as curriculum major, semester unit, college and non-college, curriculum, practical arts, laboratory science and the like.

Summary.

Educational guidance is a process of assisting the **individual** to match his capacities with school opportunities, and is chiefly concerned with: (1) school orientation; (2) student programming with choice of electives; (3) graduation requirements; (4) college entrance requirements; (5) further educational opportunities; (6) better study habits; and (7) miscellaneous educational information. Responsibility for educational guidance is the function of faculty, students, parents and sometimes selected specialists.

Suggested References.

Educational Policies Commission, *Education for All American Youth*, Washington, D. C.: National Education Association, 1944. Chapter 3.

Cole, Luella, and Ferguson, Jessie M., *Student's Guide to Efficient Study*. New York: Farrar & Rinehart, 1935.

Cox, W. L., and Duff, John C., *Guidance by the Classroom Teacher*. New York: Prentice-Hall, Inc., 1941.   Chapter 6.

Hamrin, Shirley A., and Erickson, C. E., *Guidance in the Secondary School*. New York: D. Appleton-Century Company, 1939.

Paterson, Donald C., et al., *Student Guidance Techniques*. New York: McGraw-Hill Book Company, 1938. Pp. 257-270.

Schmaelzle, O. I., Editor, *A Guide to Counseling*. San Francisco: San Francisco Public Schools, 1944.   Part II.

Smith, Samuel and Littlefield, Arthur W., *Best Methods of Study*. New York: Barnes and Noble, Inc., 1938.

Webster, B. C., *Guidance for the High School Pupil*. Montreal: McGill University press, 1940.   Parts I and IV.

SECTION E. COUNSELING THE HIGH SCHOOL STUDENT REGARDING VOCATIONAL PLANS.

Purpose: *and occupational infor-*

Vocational Planning.

Vocational planning is that process which helps the individual to make an objective appraisal of himself, and an organized analysis of employment demands and placement opportunities. Taking into account these two kinds of information, the individual can make more effective plans for training and placement and for achieving satisfaction in the world of work.

Description:

The Need for Vocational Planning.

The student's need for vocational planning is most intensified just before entering and before leaving high school. Before enrollment in senior high school, students should make tentative vocational plans so that a program of studies may be chosen in harmony with the broad area of occupational interest.

Previous to leaving high school, the student should be counseled regarding further training, successful ways of getting and holding a job and achieving satisfaction over a period of time.

Vocational Counseling Should be a Cooperative Process.

1. Every teacher should be aware of his responsibility for doing vocational counseling.

2. Counselors should not only assist students directly but also participate in an in-service guidance training program for teachers.

3. Administrators should arrange schedules with specific reference to teachers who have the requisites for vocational counseling.

4. Students will receive more effective vocational counseling when they participate cooperatively in the process.

5. Carefully selected specialists may be invited to give occupational information on Career Day or at the place of work. (See "Suggestions for Career Day" Los Angeles County Superintendent of Schools Office Research and Guidance Monograph No. 15075.)

Assisting Students in Making Vocational Plans.

The following factors must be analyzed in detail to set up an effective method of establishing a system to assist the students in vocational planning:

a. Gathering data regarding the student.

b. Giving information about occupational opportunities.

c. Matching personal assets with the requirements of vocational opportunities.

1. Data needed regarding the student.

   a. Give and interpret individual and group tests. (For a complete discussion of such tests, see Chapter II, Section A.)

   b. Obtain appraisal of student by teachers of industrial arts, vocational and special subjects.

   c. Analyze personal-social data. (See Counseling Process, Chapter V, Sections B and C.)

   d. Assist the student to interpret data regarding himself.

2. Information needed about occupational opportunities.

   a. General information regarding job requirements.

      (1) Training.

      (2) Experience.

      (3) Aptitude—physical, mental, emotional and social.

      (4) Punctuality.

    (5) Unavoidable hazards and work annoyances—dust, smoke, fumes, heat or cold, humidity, grease and dirt.

    (6) Demands—physical, visual, mental.

    (7) Responsibilities for equipment, product and safety of others.

    (8) Credentials — licenses, Social Security, union membership.

    (9) Clock hours or seasons of work.

    (10) Place or mobility of work.

    (11) Terms peculiar to the occupation.

b. General information regarding broad areas of employment that have transferable skills and that require related knowledges and information, i.e., job families.

c. Specific information regarding fields of work.

    (1) Trends in various fields.

    (2) Trends in various industries.

    (3) Pay rates.

    (4) Opportunities for advancement.

    (5) Job specifications.

    (6) Benefits, such as sickness and accident, vacation, pension and others.

3. How can personal assets be matched with the requirements of vocational opportunities?

a. Provide opportunity for try-out work experience.

b. Compare student's interest with requirements of occupational fields and ability with the various employment levels in the field.

c. Recognize the importance of the individual's personal drive even though it is difficult to evaluate.

d. Assist student through the counseling process.

e. Realize that the results of any matching of individual with job may vary from time to time, as new information regarding the student or the occupational field becomes available.

4. Information about occupational opportunities can be obtained by two chief methods:————

   a. By first-hand experience, such as:
      (1) Field trips to industries.
      (2) Interviews with representatives from various occupations.
      (3) Career Day at school.
      (4) Work experience.
      (5) Exploratory courses.

   b. From literature, such as:
      (1) *Dictionary of Occupational Titles.* Washington, D. C.: United States Employment Service.
      (2) *Bulletins of Occupational Information and Guidance Service.* Washington, D. C.: United State Office of Education.
      (3) Publications of Science Research Associates, Chicago, Illinois.
      (4) *Monographs on Careers.* Chicago: Institute of Research.
      (5) *Occupations.* Vocational Guidance Journal; New York: National Vocational Guidance Association.
      (6) *Occupational Information: A Bibliography of Books, Pamphlets, Periodicals and Film Titles.* Division of Research and Guidance, Monograph No. 13101; Los Angeles 12: Los Angeles County Superintendent of Schools.
      (7) Data from United States Census.
      (8) Trade magazines and current occupational

information bulletins.

    (9) Management organization publications.
       (a) United States Chamber of Commerce.
       (b) National Association of Manufacturers.
    (10) Literature regarding Labor organizations.
       (a) American Federation of Labor.
       (b) Congress of Industrial Organization.

5. Matching personal assets with the requirements of vocational opportunities.
   a. Interests of the student will indicate the area of occupational placement, and ability of the student will indicate objectively the employment level in the occupational area.
   b. It is well to remember that certain personal assets cannot be adequately evaluated. However, this attempt at matching individuals and jobs has been very helpful in vocational planning.
   c. A suggested form is included that will partially fulfill this matching relationship. (See Student Work Sheet For Vocational Planning.)

6. Action Required by School Personnel.
   a. Cooperation with business and industry.
      (1) Joint conferences with business leaders, students and teachers.
      (2) Formulation of school-work plan.
      (3) Teacher participation in education, management and labor conferences.
   b. Students should be informed regarding further training opportunities, such as:
      (1) Continuation classes.
      (2) Post-graduate courses in Commercial and Practical Arts Departments of senior high school.
      (3) Junior colleges.

      (4) Day and evening adult classes.

      (5) Trade schools.

      (6) Commercial schools.

      (7) Colleges and universities.

      (8) Libraries and museums.

      (9) Correspondence courses.

    (10) Apprenticeship and on-the-job training.

c. Follow-up records should be developed and maintained in the cumulative file of the former student. These should include:

      (1) Employment record.

      (2) Education beyond high school.

      (3) Other appropriate information regarding each student. (A suggested form for securing the above information is found on the "Former Student Information" sheet.)

Supplemental Information Helpful to Students.

1. How to get a job.

    a. Decide upon a job area preferred.

    b. List all employers in job area from telephone book, city directory and other sources.

    c. Write letter of application or make appointment for an employment interview.

    d. Outline what applicant will say to prospective employer.

      (1) Include name, age, grade in school, courses pursued, special skills developed and other job experience.

      (2) Include also location of home, available transportation to work, freedom from distracting obligations.

(Continued an page 152)

STUDENT WORK SHEET FOR VOCATIONAL PLANNING

(To be used at completion of vocational instruction)

Name _____ Occupation Being Investigated _____ Date _____

INSTRUCTIONS: Choosing a lifetime occupation is an active process in which you must play the major role. You must determine the degree to which your personal assets match job requirements. This should be done in cooperation with the counselor or teacher. Fill in the three columns below as completely as you can. In the Rank Column, center, indicate the extent to which your personal assets match the job requirements. Circle one of the numbers 1, 2, 3, 4, or 5 in each space. An encircled (1) represents very high suitability for the job, an encircled (5) represents very low suitability for the job.

RANK

Circle extent to which personal assets match
job requirements, for example: 5 4 (3) 2 1

JOB REQUIREMENTS	5 4 (3) 2 1	PERSONAL ASSETS
1. Interests required.	5 4 3 2 1	To what extent am I interested in this job?
2. Abilities or aptitudes required.	5 4 3 2 1	Do I have the necessary abilities and aptitudes?
3. Amount and kind of education required.	5 4 3 2 1	Do I have it, or can I get it?
4. Number of employees required.	5 4 3 2 1	Will there be a vacancy for me?
5. Time, place, hours and regularity of work.	5 4 3 2 1	Will I be satisfied with time and place of work?
6. Remuneration and advancement.	5 4 3 2 1	Will I be satisfied with this salary and prospect for advancement?
7. Physique and health required.	5 4 3 2 1	Do I have the size, strength and health to be successful?
8. Responsibility for equipment, production, personnel.	5 4 ½ 3 2 1	Can I carry the necessary responsibility?
9. Personal associations required.	5 4 3 2 1	Will I be happy with my working associates?
10. Mental and Physical hazards.	5 4 3 2 1	Can I stand the strain of this work?

Total average rank................ (To find the total average rank, add the encircled numbers and divide by the number of items rated. If the job is suitable for you, your total average rank should be less than 3 and preferably 2 or below.)

FORMER STUDENT INFORMATION

Name..Course.....................Year.......

Address..Phone.......................

Married.......Single.......Dependents...

Part A. ESTIMATE OF THE VALUE OF SCHOOL TRAINING.
(Confidential)...

1. **What Can The School Do to Help You Now?**
....

....

2. **If You Were a High School Student Again, What Recommendations Do You Have for Improving the School?**
....

....

3. **Which of Your Extracurricular Activities Have Proved Most Valuable to You?**
....

....

4. **What Subjects Have Given You the Greatest Help and Why?**...

....

Part B. EDUCATION BEYOND HIGH SCHOOL

DATES From	To	School	Course	Credit	Remarks

Part C. EMPLOYMENT RECORD

Job	DATES From	To	Employer	Address	How Job Was Obtained

EMPLOYMENT RECORD (Cont'd.)

Job	Kind of Work Done	Pay Rate	Reason for Leaving	Remarks

e. Wear appropriate dress for the job interview.

f. Keep a check sheet showing letters of application written, interview scheduled and completed, follow-ups, applications to be made.

2. How to hold a job.

a. Perform job duties satisfactorily.

(1) Sufficient knowledge of job.

(2) Sufficient energy and skills.

b. Get along agreeably with employer.

(1) Be prompt and regular in working schedule.

(2) Know and follow company policies.

(3) Be diplomatic and follow instructions.

c. Get along agreeably with fellow workers.

(1) Give and accept cooperation.

(2) Do your share.

d. Understand the whole job.

(1) Learn about other processes which make the completed product, in addition to your own operations.

(2) Understand and practice proper industrial relations.

3. How to achieve satisfaction on the job.

a. Develop liking for activities demanded by job.

b. Cultivate satisfying social relationships.

c. Make use of personal growth possibilities connected with job.

Function

Summary.

An adequate vocational guidance program should assist each student in wise vocational planning and adjustment, training, job placement, follow-up and job satisfaction. School personnel, students, business, professions, management, labor and industry should cooperate in the program. Better vocational planning and occupational adjustment may be achieved by the use of tests, personal-social data, occupational information, guidance classes or units, a system of record keeping and individual counseling. Continuous checking should reveal the extent to which the vocational guidance program is achieving its purpose. *Stop* END

Suggested References.

Bingham, Walter V., *Aptitudes and Aptitude Testing.* New York: Harper and Brothers, 1937. Chapter 9.

California State Reconstruction and Reemployment Commission, *How Many Jobs for Californians?* Sacramento 14: The Commission, 1944.

Census Bureau Publications. Washington 25, D. C.: Superintendent of Documents.

Forrester, Gertrude, *Methods of Vocational Guidance.* Boston: D. C. Heath and Company, 1944. Chapters 1-12.

Myers, George E., *Principles and Techniques of Vocational Guidance.* New York: McGraw-Hill Book Company, 1941.

CHAPTER VI

MODERN GUIDANCE MATERIALS

SECTION A. BOOKS AND SUPPLEMENTARY READING MATERIALS EVALUATED AS TO READING DIFFICULTY LEVEL.

There is a need, in every school, for an adequate supply of guidance books and supplementary reading materials so that:

1. Teacher time and energy may be efficiently expended.
2. The guidance system may be based on a sound informational foundation to which constant reference can be made.
3. The guidance staff may be acquainted with the new developments relating to vocational opportunities and the type of training required in each vocational area.
4. Individual guidance needs may be adequately met.

Importance of Providing Materials for Students on Various Reading Difficulty Levels.

Many high school students have very little difficulty with reading. On the other hand, a considerable number of students, equally intelligent, have serious difficulty with this process. Research has shown that reading disability is one of the important contributing factors to personal maladjustment. Many students avoid literature and other subjects that draw heavily on reading content. It is apparent, therefore, that adequate guidance in the reading process requires a variety of evaluated materials at the secondary level, because:

1. There is a wide range of interests in each class.
2. There is a wide range of ability in each class.
3. One set of textbooks is inadequate to meet the varied abilities and interests of all the students.

What Materials Are Available.

The ordinary school or classroom library is often devoid of adequate books and reading materials which have been evaluated as to reading difficulty level. There is a wealth of materials to be obtained with a little time and effort. These materials may be classified into (1) teacher lists and helps pertaining to evaluated materials, and (2) student materials which have been evaluated and classified as to interest area.

1. Teacher helps and lists pertaining to evaluated materials:

   a. California State Department of Education, *List of High School Textbooks.* Bulletin, Vol. XVI, No. 2; Sacramento: Library and Courts Building, August, 1947.

   b. Los Angeles City Superintendent of Schools, *Books Evaluated by Means of the Vocabulary Grade Placement Formula.* Los Angeles 12: Los Angeles City Schools, March, 1937.

   c. _____, *The Improvement of Reading in Secondary Schools*, School Publication No. 358; Los Angeles 12: Los Angeles City Schools, 1940.

   d. Los Angeles County Superintendent of Schools, "The Reading Process." Bulletin No. 8093; Los Angeles 12: Division of Research and Guidance, May, 1940.

   e. _____, "How May Secondary Teachers Distinguish Between a Case of Severe Reading Difficulty and One of Low Mental Development?" Bulletin No. 9049; Los Angeles 12:

Division of Research and Guidance, May, 1942.

f. _____, "Pleasure - Reading Books for Slow-Reading Groups at the Junior and Senior High School Level." Bulletin E-18; Los Angeles 12: Division of Secondary Education, September, 1941.

g. _____, "Textbooks and Instructional Materials Evaluated." Bulletin No. 6169; Los Angeles 12: Division of Research and Guidance, 1938.

h. _____, "Textbooks and Instructional Materials Evaluated." Bulletin No. 7130; Los Angeles 12: Division of Research and Guidance, April, 1939.

i. _____, "Textbooks and Instructional Materials Evaluated." Bulletin No. 8010; Los Angeles 12: Division of Research and Guidance, August, 1939.

j. Nolan, Esther Grace, "Reading Difficulty Versus Low Mentality," *California Journal of Secondary Education*, 17:34-39; January, 1942.

k. _____, "Training Teachers to Use Measurement as a Guidance Tool, *Education*, 66:436-442, March, 1946.

l. "Pupil Guidance in the Classroom," *Los Angeles School Journal*, Vol. XXI, No. 29, April 25, 1938.

m. Strang, Ruth, et al., *Gateways to Readable Books.* New York: H. W. Wilson Company, 1944.

n. "Supplement to Pupil Guidance in the Classroom," *Los Angeles School Journal*, Vol. XXIII, No. 29, April 29, 1940.

o. Additional bibliography listed in "Reading Process,"

Los Angeles County Superintendent of Schools, Bulletin No. 8093.

2. Student materials which have been evaluated and classified: See preceding list, references b, f, g, h, i and m.

Using Evaluated Reading Materials.

1. When a classroom teacher has available the results of intelligence and achievement tests and an interest inventory of the class, he will be aware of the individual interests and capacities of the students.

   a. He will know, for example, that Tom is highly interested in radio, and in attempting to motivate Tom to greater interest in reading, he will provide free reading materials and supplementary books in the radio field. This can be done, even though the boy may have only seventh grade reading ability. One such book might be: *Radio from Start to Finish*, by Franklin Reck (New York: Crowell Publishing Company, 1942). This book has been evaluated at approximately sixth grade reading difficulty.

   b. The teacher will also be aware of the special interest of Mary, who loves to make things with her hands such as inexpensive gifts for her friends. Even though Mary's reading ability is only about the fifth grade level, materials can still be chosen to suit Mary's needs. One such book the teacher can secure for this girl's free reading might be *Holiday Handicraft*, by Nina Jordan, (New York: Harcourt-Brace Publishing Company, 1938). This book has been evaluated at approximately fourth grade reading difficulty.

   c. The teacher in securing free reading materials for Jack, who reads at twelfth grade level and who is interested in international relations, could give him, for example, the book *Pacific Relations*, by W. G. Hoffman (New York: McGraw-Hill Book Company, 1936). This book has been evaluated at approximately eleventh grade level.

2. A reading club often proves more effective and popular with students than a class designated as remedial reading.

3. The display of attractive, easy-reading books and highly colored book jackets about the room or library often entices some students with reading antagonisms, to pick up a book in their specific interest field. Subsequently they often learn to overcome their dislikes, and come to enjoy reading.

4. A reading room with open book shelves, racks for booklets, tables for magazines, attractive curtains, pictures, and plants or flowers, with movable chairs and tables, also does much to overcome antipathy for reading.

Summary.

One effective means for guidance at the secondary level is an adequate supply of reading material carefully evaluated as to reading difficulty level. Careful choice of reading material will help meet the wide range of ability and the varying interests of each class. These reading materials may be made available and attractive to students through the use of book clubs, special book displays and the like.

SECTION B. TRAINING OF GUIDANCE WORKERS IN THE USE OF AUDIO-VISUAL AIDS.

Audio-Visual Aids in Guidance.

Every student needs assistance in securing accurate information that will aid him in (1) making a wise vocational choice and in (2) achieving satisfactory personal-social adjustment to his environment. Since many students learn most readily through what they see and hear, audio-visual aids offer an effective and interesting means of guidance.

The rapidly expanding field of audio-visual aids offers an opportunity for guidance workers to accomplish results that would be difficult to obtain as effectively by other means. In this field, the following items are available to strengthen the guidance program:

1. Movies—sound and silent.

2. Slides.

3. Film strips.

4. Records and transcriptions.

5. Radio programs (Monthly Bulletin "Listen" may be secured from the Division of Audio-Visual Education).

6. Pictures.

7. Charts, diagrams and graphs (From Division of Research and Guidance).

8. Models—working and scale.

The Division of Audio-Visual Education of the Office of Los Angeles County Superintendent of Schools has published the following catalogs:

"Visual Aids Catalog for Junior and Senior High Schools," 16 mm. sound and silent films, film strips, Kodachrome slides. Bulletin Special No. 22, September, 1943.

"Supplement to Visual Aids Catalog for Junior and Senior High Schools." Bulletin Special No. 12:4-5, September, 1944.

"Supplement to Visual Aids Catalog for Junior and Senior High Schools." Bulletin Special No. 98:5-6, May, 1946.

"1945 Catalog of Sponsored Visual Aids for Elementary and Secondary Schools." Bulletin Special No. 67:4-5, January, 1945.

Criteria for Selection of Guidance Films.

1. Is the film technically acceptable with regard to the following?

   a. Photography

   b. Sequence

   c. Setting

   d. Sound

   e. Music

   f. Motion

2. Is the film a suitable supplement to the discussion of the guidance problem? The following factors should be considered:

   a. Is the information disclosed by the film pertinent to the guidance problem?

   b. Are the vocabulary and information suitable to the age level and interests of the group?

   c. Does the film re-enforce other visual and auditory materials that are being used in the guidance program?

Helps For Utilization of Auditory and Visual Materials.

To realize the greatest guidance value from auditory and visual aids, teachers and counselors should be trained to make them an integral part of the guidance program.

1. Teacher or counselor preparation.

   a. Preview the film.

   b. Decide how the film can best supplement the discussion of a guidance problem.

   c. Use material for definite guidance purposes, such as:

      (1) Help student to appraise his own ability.

      (2) Assist student to understand social and economic opportunities and requirements.

      (3) Counsel student to match assets with opportunities.

      (4) Facilitate adjustment.

2. Student preparation.

   a. Suggested valuable techniques for use with a guidance group.

      (1) List and discuss difficult words used in the film.

      (2) Set up definite questions to be answered by the film.

   b. Emphasis of major guidance values of film.

3. Follow-up after showing of film.

   a. Discuss to what extent the film helped students understand their assets.

   b. Check the amount of guidance information received from the film.

   c. Evaluate the film with reference to its guidance values.

Useful Audio-Visual Materials.

1. Titles of films for Orientation Purposes: (The following films are available in the Division of Audio-Visual Education, Los Angeles County Superintendent of Schools Office.)

   Agriculture.
   Aptitudes and Occupations.
   Bookkeeping and Accounting.
   Care of the New Born Baby.
   Charm and Personality.
   Cowboy Picture.
   Farming Takes Skill.
   Finding Your Life Work.
   Golden Harvest.
   Guardians of the Sea.
   Home Nursing.
   Is There Room For Us?
   I Want a Job.
   Journalism.
   Lumberman.
   Miracle in Wood.
   Newsreel.
   New Ways of Farming.
   Nursing.
   Oranges That Please.
   Photography.
   Poultry Raising.
   Silversmith.
   Teen Age Farm Hand.
   Unfinished Rainbows.
   What About Jobs?

2. Titles of Films for Occupational Adjustment.

Advanced Typing—Duplicating and Manuscript.
Advanced Typing—Short Cuts.
Aluminum Fabricating Processes.
Automotive Service.
Basic Typing—Machine Operation.
Basic Typing—Methods.
Bathing the Bed Patient.
Beds and Appliances.
Behind the Shop Drawing.
Brick and Stone Mason.
Dairy Industry.
Draftsman.
Electrician.
Engineering.
Heating and Air Conditioning.
How to Machine Aluminum.
How to Weld Aluminum.
Machinist and Toolmaker.
Of Pups and Puzzles.
Oral Medication.
Painting and Decorating.
Plumbing.
Post-Operative Care.
Radio and Television.
Selling America.
Take a Letter, Please—How to Dictate.
Temperature, Pulse and Respiration.
Twenty-four Jobs.
Underwood Typing Tips.

Welding.

Welding Operator.

Woodworker.

3. Radio.

Radio is one of the most powerful forces in molding opinion and attitudes. It is a force which carries great constructive potentiality for guidance purposes. It can be used as an excellent vehicle to make school work interesting. Radio can be used as a single instrument or in conjunction with many types of visual material. Students may listen to programs direct from the radio or recordings may be made of music, drama, literature, history, news commentaries, science programs and the like. Such recordings can be incorporated as an important addition to audio-visual materials and thus become a valuable aid in guidance.

Radio is to become even more important from a guidance point of view through the development and use of television. Schools need to be ready to capitalize on the use of this new instrument when it becomes available.

Valuable help on the use of radio may be secured from these sources:

Chase, Gilbert, *Music in Radio Broadcasting*. McGraw-Hill Book Company, New York, 1946.

Levensen, William, *Teaching Through Radio*. Farrar and Rinehart, New York, 1945.

Woeful, Norman, and Tyler, I. Keith, *Radio and the School*. World Book Company, Yonkers-on-Hudson, New York, 1945.

The American School of the Air, Columbia Broadcasting System, 485 Madison Avenue, New York 22, N. Y.

"Listen," Division of Audio-Visual Education, Office

of the County Superintendent of Schools, 808 North
Spring St., Los Angeles 12, California.

The Standard School Broadcast, 225 Bush St., San
Francisco 20, California.

The United States Office of Education, Washington, D. C.

Summary.

Guidance workers can accomplish a great deal through the
use of audio-visual aids. The use of audio-visual aids con-
serves both teacher and student time and contributes to more
effective group guidance.

SECTION C. LIBRARY OF OCCUPATIONAL INFORMATION.

A wealth of information about jobs and job opportunities
is available to the secondary school teacher and counselor.
To make the use of this material effective in the guidance program, it is necessary to have a definite plan or system for its
organization and distribution.

A good workable system for organizing occupational information involves:

Collection.

Filing.

Display.

Student Use.

Each of these processes is outlined below:

Collection of Occupational Information.

Consult the following sources:

1. Baltimore Department of Education, Division of Vocational Education, Baltimore. *Your Future Series*, 10c
   each.

2. Bellman Publishing Company, 6 Park Street, Boston 8. *Vocational-Professional Monographs*, 50c and 75c each; $25 for a series of 75 monographs.

3. Chronicle, Port Byron, New York, *Guidepost to Occupational Information*, 5c each, 10 copies or more, 3c each.

4. Commonwealth Book Company, 80 East Jackson Boulevard, Chicago 4. *Commonwealth Vocational Guidance Monographs*, single copies 75c; 25 monographs $12.75; 50 for $24.50; complete set of 75 for $35.

5. Institute of Research, 537 South Dearborn Street, Chicago 5. *Careers-Research Monographs*, each group contains about 5; cost of group is $3.75 except group A which costs $5.25. Discount given upon purchase of 5 or more groups.

6. Los Angeles County Superintendent of Schools, Los Angeles 12: Division of Research and Guidance, *Occupational Information, Revised. A Bibliography of Books, Pamphlets, Periodicals and Film Titles*, Monograph No. 16005, Sept. 1947. This bibliography also lists addresses of the major concerns which offer occupational information.

7. Morgan-Dillon and Company, 4616 North Clark Street, Chicago 40. *Success Vocational Information Monographs*, 32c each, 10 or more in one order, 30c each.

8. National Federation of Business and Professional Women's Clubs, Inc., 1819 Broadway, New York City 23. *Vocations for Women*, reprints published prior to 1944, 10c each; published 1944 to date, 15c each.

9. National Roster of Scientific and Specialized Personnel, U. S. Department of Labor, Washington 25, D. C. *Descriptions of Professions Series*, free; *Handbooks of Description of Specialized Fields*, (Supt. of Documents, Washington, D. C.); *Occupational Briefs*, (Supt. of Documents) 5c each.

10. New York State Department of Education, Guidance Bureau, Port Byron, New York. *Occupational Briefs.*

11. New York University, Washington Square, New York City 3. Occupational Index, Inc., *Occupational Abstracts,* 25c each; 10 or more, 15c each.

12. Quarrie Corporation, 35 East Wacker Drive, Chicago 1. *Vocational Monographs* (Quarrie Reference Library); currently at $1 a set (29 monographs).

13. Rochester Institute of Technology, Rochester 8, New York. *Vocational Guidance Series,* 10c each.

14. Row, Peterson and Company, Evanston, Ill. *Way of Life Series,* list price, 96c each; net price to schools and libraries, 56c each.

15. Science Research Associates, 228 South Wabash Ave., Chicago 4. *American Job Series of Occupational Monographs,* 60c each; 4 or more, 55c each; 10 or more, 45c each; 30 or more, 40c each. *Occupational Briefs,* 15c each; 50 or more, 10c each; *Occupational Reprints,* 15c each; 50 or more copies, 10c each.

16. State Board of Vocational Education, Lincoln, Nebraska. *Free and Near-Free Occupational Material,* Bulletin III, 1946.

17. United States Department of Commerce, Bureau of Foreign and Domestic Commerce. *Industrial Series,* (Supt. of Documents, Washington 25, D. C.)

18. United States Department of Labor, Washington 25, D. C. Labor market information for USES Counselling, *Industry Series,* 1945, free.

19. United States Department of Labor, Bureau of Labor Statistics. *Occupational Outlook Division Series,* (Supt. of Documents), 10c each.

20. United States Department of Labor, Division of Occupational Analysis. *Individual Job Descriptions*, (Supt. of Documents), some free, some 5c.

21. United States Department of Labor, Women's Bureau. *Outlook for Women in Occupations in Medical Services*, (Supt. of Documents, Washington 25, D. C.), 10c each.

22. United States Employment Service. *Dictionary of Occupational Titles and Codes*, Parts I, II, III, IV and Supplements (Supt. of Documents, Washington 25, D. C.)

23. United States Office of Education. *Guidance Leaflets*, (Supt. of Documents), 5c each.

24. United States War Dept. *Occupational Briefs*, (Supt. of Documents), 5c each.

25. United States War Man Power Commission, Washington 25, D. C. *Industrial Job Family Set, Occupation Job Family Set, Vocational Monographs, Labor Market Monthly, Area Statements.*

26. Vocational Guidance Manuals, Inc., 45 West 45th Street, New York City 19. *Vocational Guidance Manuals*, $1, $1.25 each, 1946.

27. Western Personnel Service, 130 Raymond Avenue, Pasadena 1, Calif. *Occupational Briefs*, 1941-44, 25c each.

Filing of Occupational Information.

1. Books may be catalogued in the library's regular filing and marking system.

2. Pamphlets may be filed alphabetically according to major job areas.

3. Periodical articles may be listed with annotations in a **card index** file.

4. Clippings and other perishable material may be

mounted on cards and deposited in the pamphlet file. If left loose, they should be filed in a clippings file.

5. Each book, pamphlet, article and clipping should be represented by a reference in the **card index** file.

   a. A separate **card index** file may, or may not, be made for occupational information materials.

   b. The index card should contain:
   Occupational field.
   Title.
   Author and publisher.
   Date, number of pages.
   Library number.
   A brief annotation.

6. Film titles should be indexed with annotations and the addresses of film depositories.

7. College bulletins and catalogs should be properly indexed and kept on special shelves or in occupational reading rooms.

8. Special, private and technical school information should include rating of school, courses available, degrees offered and the like.

Display of Occupational Information.

Salesmanship is needed in the display of occupational information just as surely as it is needed in the selling of such basic necessities as food, clothing and houses. Counselors, librarians and teachers should have training in ways to impress students with the need for more information concerning jobs, and the way to display materials in an appealing manner. The following devices have been used in various schools:

1. Special library shelves labeled "Vocations" or "Occupational Information."

2. Career rooms where many reading and visual materials are easily available for study.

3. Special tables where key materials are rotated from timo to time.

4. "Notion" counter displays in the line of library traffic similar to the notion displays used near the cash register in markets. Blueprints for such a display have been developed by Dr. Alfred Lewerenz, Los Angeles City Schools, Evaluation Section.

5. Bulletin board displays of book jackets, pictures, graphs, charts, pictograms, film titles, clippings, magazine articles and small pamphlets.

6. Posters which give occupational information or induce the student to seek information.

7. Feature columns or box items in the school paper which draw attention to occupational materials.

8. New and frequently sought after materials may be announced through special or regular bulletins, or by public address system.

9. Bibliography sheets, general lists by the librarian and special lists by the commercial teacher.

Student Use of Occupational Materials.

Occupational materials which remain neatly arranged in library files are worthless to students; they are valuable only in proportion to their use. A few methods, such as the following, to increase the circulation and use of occupational materials, should be stressed:

1. Frequently used materials may be placed on the overnight list.

2. Classes may be transferred to the library for a period so that students may examine and check out occupational materials.

3. Sets of specialized materials (pertaining to woodworking, metalcraft, graphic art and the like) may be sent to the classroom and checked out by the teacher.

4. A "mobile occupational library" has been used in some schools to carry miscellaneous materials to the classroom. For directions concerning construction of such a mobile unit, see John O. Hershey, "A Mobile Occupational Library in the Classroom," *Occupations* 24:91, November, 1945.

5. Classroom teachers may make assignments which involve the reading of occupational materials.

Finally, the whole purpose for collecting, filing, displaying and using of occupational information is to help students make more suitable vocational plans.

Summary.

Much material concerning jobs is available. Effective occupational information service involves collection, filing, display and student use of materials pertaining to jobs.

SECTION D. BASIC REFERENCES FOR GUIDANCE WORKERS.

The books listed below will help teachers, counselors and administrators with their common guidance problems. No attempt has been made to compile the many books and pamphlets which deal with specific and unique situations. The number of books in the list has been strictly limited as a means of making the references suitable for guidance workers with little reading time. A more extended bibliography has been placed at the end of this handbook.

Bacher, O. R., and Berkowitz, G. J., *School Courses and Related Careers*. Chicago: Science Research Associates, 1945.

Bell, Howard M., *Matching Youth and Jobs*. Washington 6, D. C.: American Council on Education, 1940.

Bingham, Walter V., *Aptitudes and Aptitude Testing*. New York: Harper and Brothers, 1937.

Bingham, Walter V., and Moore, Bruce V., *How to Interview*. New York: Harper and Brothers, 1941.

Brewer, John M., et al., *History of Vocational Guidance*. New York: Harper and Brothers, 1942.

Cox, W. L., and Duff, John Carr, *Guidance by the Classroom Teacher*. New York: Prentice-Hall, Inc., 1941.

Darley, John G., *Testing and Counseling in the High School Guidance Program*. Chicago: Science Research Associates, 1942.

Forrester, Gertrude, *Methods of Vocational Guidance*. Boston: D. C. Heath and Company, 1944

Germane, Charles E., and Germane, Edith G., *Personnel Work in High School*. Chicago: Silver Burdett Company, 1941.

Hamrin, Shirley A., and Erickson, Clifford E., *Guidance in the Secondary School*. New York: D. Appleton-Century Company, 1939.

Jones, Arthur J., *Principles of Guidance*. New York: McGraw-Hill Book Company, 1945.

Kefauver, Grayson N., and Hand, Harold C., *Appraising Guidance in Secondary Schools*. New York: The Macmillan Company, 1941.

Lefever, D. Welty, et al., *Principles and Techniques of Guidance*. New York: The Ronald Press Company, 1941.

Myers, George E., *Principles and Techniques of Vocational Guidance*. New York: McGraw-Hill Book Company, 1941.

Reed, Anna Y., *Guidance and Personnel Services in Education*. Ithaca, New York: Cornell University Press, 1944.

Rogers, Carl R., *Counseling and Psychotherapy*. Boston: Houghton Mifflin Company, 1942.

Smith, Charles M., and Roos, Mary M., *Guide to Guidance*. New York: Prentice-Hall, Inc., 1942.

Strang, Ruth, *Pupil Personnel and Guidance*. New York: The Macmillan Company, 1940.

Super, Donald E., *Dynamics of Vocational Adjustment*. New York: Harper and Brothers, 1942.

Traxler, Arthur E., *Techniques of Guidance*. New York: Harper and Brothers, 1945.

Williamson, E. G., and Darley, J. E., *Student Personnel Work*. New York: McGraw-Hill Book Company, 1937.

Williamson, E. G., and Hahn, M. E., *Introduction to High School Counseling*. New York: McGraw-Hill Book Company, 1940.

Yale, John R., Editor, *Frontier Thinking in Guidance*. Chicago: Science Research Associates, 1945.

United States Office of Education, *Occupational Information and Guidance Series*. Washington 25, D. C.: Superintendent of Documents.

CHAPTER VII

TECHNIQUES FOR IMPROVING PROFESSIONAL GROWTH IN GUIDANCE

Professional Growth in Guidance.

An in-service training program should lead to continuous professional growth in guidance activities for all teachers, counselors and administrators. Guidance workers learn most effectively by participating in the guidance program. Activities such as the following will promote professional growth in service:

1. Cooperative planning for guidance.
2. Group and individual guidance activities.
3. Administrative devices for stimulating in-service growth.
4. Further study of guidance objectives, principles, procedures and research findings.
5. Better acquaintance with the community.

In-Service Training Is Needed by All Guidance Workers.

Continuous participation in guidance activities is essential if guidance workers are to improve their services. No staff of a teacher-training institution can anticipate the guidance needs of individual communities, nor can they predict social, economic and political changes which will affect all future guidance programs. Further training must, therefore, be provided on the job. Individual school systems have faculties with varying degrees of training: some hold emergency credentials only; others have minimum certification with no pre-training in guidance; while still others have come from sections of the country where little or no stress has been laid upon guidance services.

Transfer teachers will need to learn about the local school, the community and the guidance organization. All guidance workers should keep abreast of late research in areas of adolescent growth, learning and adjustment.

For successful adjustment of adolescents, every guidance worker must expand his information concerning new procedures, recent materials and changing community resources. Guidance workers should understand the aspects of an ever-changing community and be especially familiar with such problems as:

1. Business and industrial opportunities.

2. Educational requirements and opportunities.

3. Civic duties and responsibilities.

4. Better physical and mental health practices.

5. Recreational needs and facilities.

6. Home building and family relations.

7. Changing social and moral customs.

Continuous Professional Growth—A Cooperative Enterprise.

All school personnel should plan and participate in the professional growth program.

1. The in-service training program should be planned **by** the entire staff—administrators, supervisors, teachers, counselors, registrar, librarian, school nurse or physician, secretaries and playground director.

    a. Participation in formulating plans enables each member to express needs connected with his task.

    b. Cooperation in planning by each member makes him more competent in performing assigned duties.

    c. Initiation of planning for in-service growth is the responsibility of the administration.

2. **All members** of the educational staff should participate in the in-service training program.

    a. Activities planned for each member should be suitable to his particular function; for example, the administrator should study ways of arranging situations which promote guidance functions; the clerk should study problems connected with the recording of confidential data, and the like.

    b. Members of the staff having common needs and duties such as testing or interviewing should participate in cooperative group activities.

How to Improve In-Service Training.

Ways of promoting continuous professional growth in guidance activities should include:

    (1) Guidance worker induction and orientation.
    (2) Cooperative planning for professional growth.
    (3) Group and individual guidance activities.
    (4) Administrative devices for stimulating in-service growth.

Specific suggestions regarding the four points above follow:

1. Induction and orientation of guidance workers.

    a. New guidance workers need orientation to the school and the community as a part of the in-service training program. Each in-coming guidance worker should receive the following:

     (1)   Information about school plant, the educational program and faculty organization.

     (2)   Acquaintance with community privileges, responsibilities and opportunities.

     (3)   Guidance data concerning students.

     (4)   Assignment to school and community committees.

     (5)   Invitation to social and professional events.

     (6)   Suggestions concerning professional and lay organizations.

     (7)   Reference to services from county and state offices.

     (8)   A feeling of security and importance in the school.

2. Cooperative planning for professional growth.

   a. Teachers, teacher-counselors and others who perform similar guidance functions should meet to plan group activities.

   b. The clerk, nurse and principal who have relatively different functions, should plan their own in-service growth programs and submit them to the entire staff for suggestions and discussion.

   c. Some in-service plans may be individually formulated, but should be cooperatively approved.

3. Group and individual participation in guidance activities.

   a. Typical group activities.

     (1)   Guidance conferences, workshops, institutes and faculty meetings.

     (2)   After-school clinics regarding student problems.

     (3)   Joint teacher-parent study groups dealing with guidance.

    (4) Cooperative reviews of research by faculty committees.

    (5) Committee evaluation of instructional outcomes.

    (6) Group study of comparative guidance programs.

    (7) Staff responsibility for interpreting the guidance program to community. (See Chapter VIII.)

b. Typical individual activities.

    (1) Development of professional attitude especially with reference to the handling of confidential student data.

    (2) Preparation of case studies.

    (3) Administration of a testing program. (See Chapter II, Section A.)

    (4) Interpretation of test results.[1]

    (5) Assistance with student government.

    (6) Collection of occupational information.

    (7) Observation of student behavior and preparation of anecdotal records.

    (8) Maintenance of cumulative records.

    (9) Practice in counseling and interviewing.

  (10) Study and application of principles in handbooks, bulletins and other printed materials.

  (11) Individually conducted research in guidance problems.

  (12) Volunteer service to churches, Y. M. C. A., Y. W. C. A., Junior Red Cross, Scouts, Campfire, Woodcraft Rangers and other youth groups.

  (13) Membership in local, state and national guidance organizations, such as:

      (a) American Educational Research Association.

[1] Esther Grace Nolan, "Training Teachers to Use Measurement as a Guidance Tool." *Education*, 66: 436-442, March, 1946.

      (b) American Psychological Association.

      (c) California Educational Research and Guidance Association, Southern Section.

      (d) Los Angeles County Research and Guidance Discussion Group.

      (e) Los Angeles County Secondary Guidance Group.

      (f) National Society for Mental Hygiene.

      (g) National Vocational Guidance Association.

      (h) Society for Research in Child Development.

(14) Additional university work in guidance courses.

(15) Observation of guidance programs in other schools.

(16) Selection of avocation and recreation.

(17) Vacation work in business, industry or agriculture.

(18) Acquaintance with counseling procedures in business, employment services, Veterans' Administration, and the like.

(19) Teaching in guidance courses and workshops.

(20) Subscription to local papers, bulletins and pamphlets.

(21) Library review of historical books, pictures, doccuments, surveys and reports concerning the local community.

(22) Current surveys of occupational, educational and recreational opportunities.

(23) Cooperation with community guidance agencies.

(24) Membership on committee working with parents on youth problems.

(25)   Attendance at forums, rallies, games and picnics.

(26)   Work as director of playground or summer camp.

4   How the administration can stimulate in-service growth in guidance activities.

Administrators can do much to set the stage for in-service training. They can initiate, stimulate and guide the program. The administration should devise a system of incentives and rewards to stimulate in-service growth in guidance activities. The following devices will help:

a. Inviting guidance consultants from state, county or university.

b. Providing salary increments based upon evidences of professional growth in guidance activities, such as:

(1)   Added responsibilities for testing and counseling.

(2)   Increased use of case study method.

(3)   Advanced university study.

(4)   Publication of research in guidance.

c. Advancing efficient guidance workers within the school system.

d. Publicizing or displaying teacher-prepared guidance materials.

e. Providing adequate time and proper place in the school for guidance.

f. Making available complimentary tuitions and guidance workshop opportunities for teachers and counselors.

g. Recognizing and expressing appreciation for staff members who have rendered outstanding guidance services.

h. Increasing status or salary for non-certificated personnel who demonstrate proficiency in helping to promote guidance services.

Methods of Checking the Effectiveness of the In-Service Program.

Evaluation of the in-service training program involves appraisal of the degree to which the needs and objectives of the program are being achieved. A check list form to be used in evaluating guidance services has been included in Chapter IX.

Summary.

Continuous professional growth in guidance activities is essential because schools have individual guidance needs, faculties vary in their pre-training and changes are continuous in all communities. Guidance workers need (1) to keep abreast of research, (2) to utilize the most effective guidance techniques and materials, (3) to cooperate with the total educational program, and (4) to apply basic guidance principles as well as new research findings to changing community needs.

All school personnel should participate cooperatively according to their respective ability, training and responsibilities. Guidance activities for in-service growth include (1) guidance worker orientation, (2) cooperative planning, (3) group and individual participation in guidance activities and (4) administrative devices for stimulating in-service growth.

Frequent check should be made to determine to what extent participation in guidance activities is resulting in professional growth.

Suggested References.

Group Planning in Education. 1945 Yearbook, Department of Supervision and Curriculum Development; Washington 6, D. C.: National Education Association, 1945.

Harap, Henry, et al., *The Changing Curriculum.* New York: D. Appleton-Century Company, 1937, Chapter XII.

Mental Health in the Classroom. Thirteenth Yearbook, Department of Supervisors and Directors of Instruction; Washington 6, D. C.: National Education Association, 1941.

Nolan, Esther Grace, "Training Teachers to Use Measurement as a Guidance Tool," *Education,* 66: 436-442, March, 1946.

Traxler, Arthur E., *Techniques of Guidance.* New York: Harper and Brothers, 1945. P. 343.

Troyer, Maurice E., and Pace, Robert C., *Evaluation in Teacher Education.* Washington, D. C.: American Council on Education, 1944. Chapters VIII and IX.

CHAPTER VIII

TECHNIQUES FOR INTERPRETING THE GUIDANCE PROGRAM

Guidance as used in the modern school must be continuously interpreted to the community for several reasons:

1. Most individuals in the community did not have direct personal experience with a guidance program when they attended school.

2. Interpretation of the guidance program will help parents to understand the characteristics of their adolescent children.

3. Community interest and understanding of the guidance program will result in more adequate financial support.

4. Schools need the understanding and cooperation of parents and the community to make the guidance program most effective.

5. Taxpayers are entitled to a full explanation of, and accounting for, all educational services rendered.

What Is Meant by Interpretation of the Guidance Program?

Interpretation of the guidance program is a process involving school personnel, parents and the community. Interpretation is the means for arriving at a mutual understanding of the purposes and progress of the guidance program.

Interpretation will entail many different techniques and activities, and will involve the giving of information to bring about favorable attitudes and community support.

The following principles of interpretation need to be kept in mind:

1. There must be something worth interpreting.
2. Facts should be the basis of all publicity.
3. The educational program should be clearly stated.
4. It is not safe to try to convince the public that any system is perfect.
5. Educational interpretation is a two-way process.
6. The attention of the public should be called to the work of the schools and the problems of education, and not to the Superintendent or the Board of Education.
7. Coordination must be systematically provided.
8. Sound publicity recognizes various groups and interests in the community.
9. Effective educational interpretation must be based upon an adequate understanding of the community forces which may be operating outside of the school's program.
10. Continuous verification and checking of procedures are essential.

Interpretation of the guidance program is a two-way process between the following groups:

1. Interpretation to and by the student.
2. Interpretation to and by the school personnel.
3. Interpretation to and by the parents.
4. Interpretation to and by the community and general public.

Personnel Involved in Interpretation.

1. Interpretation to and by the student.

The most important interpreter of the school program is the student, as he goes home daily, expressing certain attitudes by which his school is often judged. For this reason, it is imperative that the student understand the school's guidance program, its general purpose and techniques.

2. Interpretation to and by the school personnel.

   a. The classroom teacher.

     The classroom teacher needs to be aware of the total guidance program as well as the part he is to play in providing guidance for his class and for individual students.

     The classroom teacher, in his civic and domestic sphere, is an important agent for promotion of public interest and confidence in the school program.

   b. Special subject teachers, such as:

     Teachers of Lip Reading Classes, Speech Correction, Sex Education, Sight-saving Classes, Classes for Physically Handicapped, Developmental Classes, and the like.

     Such teachers need to realize the proper relationship of their class work to the entire educational program.

   c. Counselor, registrar or dean.

     Such a person is generally the one most closely identified with the guidance program and probably most aware of individual student problems. He should have a rather clear over-all view of the total guidance program, as well as a carefully defined picture of the part each guidance person will play.

     Because of these reasons, the counselor, registrar or dean is generally capable of helping to provide a better understanding of the guidance program, especially to new classroom teachers, and to interpret it to the community.

   d. Administrators, supervisors, coordinators and others. (See Appendix A—Organization Charts.)

(1) Superintendent or principal or his delegated authority.

(2) Vice-Principal.

(3) Special supervisors and coordinators, such as: representatives of County Office, school physician or nurse, home teacher or social worker and attendance officer.

Such persons need to be kept informed regarding the function of each phase of the guidance program.

To keep thus informed, they will have to work rather closely with the different guidance persons in the school; they will then know how well each phase is being administered.

A basic responsibility of an administrator is not only to organize an effective guidance program, but to interpret it in a manner so as to assure its acceptance. The cooperative attitude and diplomatic manner in which these persons deal with the general public, and the effective and skillful way in which the school's program is portrayed by them, are very important in securing public approval and financial support of the schools.

e. Non-certificated personnel.

The school telephone operator, secretary and custodian and other non-certificated personnel often have the opportunity to influence the general public to favorable support of the school's guidance program.

Because of this fact, it is advisable that such persons be given a general idea of the total guidance program and that they acquire a rather adequate understanding of its purposes, as a foundation for their interpretation to the community when the occasion arises.

3. Interpretation to and by the parents.

   Parents have the obligation of acquainting themselves with the purposes and methods of the guidance program not only for their own benefit but also as a means of making more adequate interpretations to the general public with whom they come in contact.

   They need to be assisted in this two-way interpretative process by those of the school personnel who are most adequately informed to facilitate a public understanding of the guidance program.

4. Interpretation to and by the community and general public.

   It is the responsibility of all school guidance persons working cooperatively together to assist in making the public aware of the ways in which the school program is organized in an attempt to meet the guidance needs of youth.

   It is important, then, that school guidance persons be aware of the possibilities provided by business and industrial leaders and key persons in the community in keeping informed as to changing community needs, so that these implications may be incorporated in the guidance program of the school.

Techniques of interpretation.

1. Interpretation to and by students.

   a. Demonstrations and auditorium programs.
      (1) School paper and annual.
      (2) Fine Arts (Music, Art, Literature, Drama, Debate).
      (3) Crafts, Shop, Hobbies and Clubs.
      (4) School broadcasts.
      (5) "Open house."

    (6) Exhibits.

    (7) Dinners and teas for parents.

  b. Competitive sports and athletic games.

  c. Participation in student body activities as officer or member.

  d. General attitude and behavior at home and in community.

2. Interpretation to and by school personnel.

  a. Reports to parents.

  b. Home visits.

  c. Field trips.

  d. Interviews and counseling.

  e. Organized group meetings in community.

    (1) Talks illustrated by coordinator or supervisor.

    (2) Talks to P.T.A.'s.

    (3) Talks to community and service groups.

  f. Faculty committees and reports.

  g. Parent-education classes.

  h. Use of visual aids.

    (1) Radio.

    (2) Films.

    (3) Models.

    (4) Charts and graphs.

  i. Career Days.

  j. Vocational and educational guidance.

  k. School column in community newspaper.

  l. Periodic bulletins.

  m. Teachers' social participation and life in community.

3. Interpretation to and by parents.

  a. Cooperation in following recommendations and

suggestions of counselors, school nurse, physician, social worker and attendance officer.

b. Punctuality in answering school letters and requests.

c. Parent communications with school.

d. Cooperation in student attendance and punctuality.

e. Conferences with counselor or other school personnel.

f. Attendance at school functions.

g. Participation in parent-education classes.

h. Attendance and participation in P.T.A.'s.

i. Interpretation to neighbors and in community contacts.

4. Interpretation to and by the community.

a. Organized group meetings in community.

(1) Service groups.

(2) Congress of Parents and Teachers.

(3) Taxpayers' Association.

(4) Municipal League.

(5) General welfare, educational and cultural groups.

b. Cooperation with school by community leaders in business, industry, professions and civic groups.

c. Attendance at school functions and auditorium programs.

d. Participation in school programs and Career Days.

e. Editorial offerings in community newspapers.

f. Community cooperation in field trips.

g. Financial cooperation in needed school expansion and development drives, projects and the like.

h. Attendance at Open House.

i. Interpretation to others regarding school program.

Interpretation Through the Use of Community Organizations and Agencies.

1. Community organizations and agencies are vital factors in any guidance program. It is necessary to remember that the school is not the only organization interested in helping the student resolve his problems, nor is the school the sole organization possessing resources capable of so doing. School guidance personnel will find it helpful to familiarize themselves with community organizations and agencies that can contribute to more effective guidance. The school should have on file a list of community organizations contributing to the guidance of youth. If this information is not available the school should conduct a survey of community resources.

2. Organizations and agencies capable of aiding in guidance.

   a. Boy Scouts of America.
   b. All Nations Boys Club.
   c. American Legion.
   d. American Red Cross.
   e. American Youth Hostels.
      (This organization specializes in providing hostels and assistance for young people interested in the out-of-doors.)
   f. Big Brother Division of the Police Department.
   g. Camp Fire Girls.
   h. Child Guidance Clinics.
   i. Church-sponsored clubs or organizations.
   j. City and County Departments of Recreation and Parks.
   k. Coordinating Councils.
      (This organization provides a composite leadership

from the many community organizations with the purpose of marshalling all resources of the community to meet specific youth problems.)

l. Girl Scouts of America.

m. Junior Police (preventive in nature).

n. Los Angeles County Agencies—Health, Parks and Recreation, Probation Departments, etc.

o. Service Clubs.

    (1) Kiwanis.

    (2) Lions.

    (3) Optimist.

    (4) Rotary International.

    (5) 20-30 Club and others.

p. Veterans' Community Center.

q. Veterans' Guidance Centers.

r. Young Men's and Young Women's Christian Associations.

Summary.

Interpretation of the guidance program to the community is necessary to bring about a better understanding and cooperation of four groups of persons: students, school personnel, parents and public.

Interpretation is the giving of information and explanation regarding the guidance program, to the end that approval of the program will bring about better adjustment for youth. Community organizations and agencies are vital factors in the interpretation of the guidance program.

Suggested References.

Fine, Benjamin, *School Publicity*. New York: Harper and Brothers, 1943.

Grinnell, J, Earle, *Interpreting the Public Schools*. New York: McGraw-Hill Book Company, 1937.

Koos, Leonard V., et al., *Administering the Secondary School*. San Francisco: American Book Company, 1940. Chapter XVII.

Moehlman, Arthur B., *School Administration*. Boston: Houghton- Mifflin Company, 1940. Chapter VIII.

"Public Relations Number," *Education*, Vol. 66, No. 10, June, 1946.

Schools in Small Communities. Seventeenth Yearbook, American Association of School Adminisrators, Washington, D. C., 1939.

"Secondary Schools and the Community," *California Journal of Secondary Education*, Vol. 21, No. 6, December 15, 1946.

CHAPTER IX

APPRAISAL OF THE GUIDANCE PROGRAM

How Effective Is the Guidance Program?

Every administrator, counselor and teacher would like an objective answer to this question. Unfortunately, it is not possible to appraise guidance with numerical exactness, for several reasons:

1. Complexity of human behavior. The school, home, church and other community agencies are constantly influencing the behavior of boys and girls. It is difficult to determine the nature and extent of the influence of any one of these agencies.

2. Determination of the effects of the guidance program as distinct from other aspects of the school program. In reality, all school experiences affect the adjustment of pupils. It is difficult to separate the influence of the counselor or teacher from the influence of the rest of the school.

3. Results of guidance often delayed. Some effects may not be apparent for several years after good counseling has occurred.

4. Quantity versus quality of guidance services. The mere presence of guidance services in the school program does not assure that they are effective in meeting the needs of students.

5. Limited reliability and validity of some guidance instruments. Although great improvements in tests and testing procedures have occurred during the past two decades, exact measurement of student adjustment has not been attained.

These difficulties in appraising the effectiveness of the guidance program are recognized as important. Nevertheless, every school administrator, counselor and teacher should endeavor to appraise the effectiveness of the total guidance program. In order to be of assistance in this process two techniques for appraisal of guidance services are presented:

1. A check list of guidance services.
2. Suggestions for evaluation of the educational program.

CHECKLIST OF GUIDANCE SERVICES

ITEM	Extent of Use Check (V) One				
	Not at all	Little	Some	Great	Very Great
I. The Place of Guidance in the Modern Secondary School.					
See Chapter I for a detailed discussion of the place of guidance in the modern secondary school.					
To what extent					
a. does the guidance program cope with the social forces which influence education? (effect upon student behavior of instability of family relationships)					
b. does the guidance program reenforce the basic purposes of education in American democracy? (self-realization, human relationships, civic responsibility, economic efficiency)......					
c. are the needs of boys and girls recognized and provided for? (recognition of the fact that girls progress through the stages of adolescent growth earlier than boys)........................					
d. are the essential characteristics of a guidance program provided? (The guidance program will be continuous and consistent from kindergarten through the secondary school)					

ITEM	Extent of Use Check (√) One				
	Not at all	Little	Some	Great	Very Great
II. Techniques for Collecting and recording Data.					
See Chapter II for a detailed discussion of techniques for collecting and recording data about students.					
To what extent					
a. is appropriate use made of such techniques for collecting and recording guidance data as the following:..........................					
1. the testing program? (the testing and evaluation program should collect evidence on all objectives of the curriculum)......................					
2. the interview? (the counselor should make careful preparation for the interview)					
3. observation and recording of student behavior? (teachers and counselors should record what the student actually does or says, not an interpretation of what is done or said)............................					
4. autobiography? (the autobiography should be used only after a period of preparation and development of student interest)					
5. questionnaire? (the questionnaire should elicit answers that are short, specific and definite)					

ITEM	Extent of Use Check (V) One				
	Not at all	Little	Some	Great	Very Great
6. case study? (a case study should be made for each student whose problems are too difficult to diagnose by group methods)					
7. cumulative records? (the cumulative record system should supply needed information about all students with a minimum of confusion or clerical work for the teacher)					

III. Techniques for the Administrator's Use of Guidance Data.

See Chapter III for a detailed discussion of techniques of administrative use of guidance data.

To what extent

a. do the superintendent and principal accept responsibility for encouraging and supporting the guidance program? (endeavor to develop a guidance philosophy with the staff)

b. do guidance personnel meet recommended standards of experience and training? (guidance personnel are selected from the staff members who are best equipped personally and in terms of training and experience) ....

ITEM	Extent of Use Check (√) One				
	Not at all	Little	Some	Great	Very Great
c. are guidance data used in promotion and placement of students? (guidance information is used in determining the optimum grade placement for individuals or groups of individuals)					
d. are guidance data used to improve curricular offerings? (consistent efforts are made to adapt the curriculum and methods of instruction to the abilities, interests and needs of students					
IV. Group Techniques for Utilizing Guidance Data.					
See Chapter IV for a discussion of group techniques for utilizing guidance data.					
To what extent..................................					
a. Is appropriate use made of the following for purposes of group guidance?					
1. core curriculum and guidance classes, such as orientation courses, home rooms, etc.?..					
2. elective and special classes, such as practical arts courses, or classes in journalism, music, art, drama, etc.?..					
3. extra-curricular activities, such as athletic organizations, club activities, student body government?......					

ITEM	Extent of Use Check (V) One				
	Not at all	Little	Some	Great	Very Great
4. special guidance events, such as field trips, Career Day, school assemblies, etc.?					

V. Techniques for Teacher and Counselor Use of Guidance Data.

See Chapter V for a detailed discussion of techniques for teacher and counselor use of guidance data.

a. Guiding Students Regarding Physical and Mental Health.

To what extent

1. are students helped to discover and correct inconsistencies in their health practices, attitudes and information? ....

2. are students enabled to discover and utilize their physical assets? ....

3. are students assisted to attain a greater measure of mental well-being?................

4. are teachers able to identify symptoms of maladjustment? ....

5. Is skilled psychological and psychiatric assistance available for the most seriously maladjusted? ....

b. Guiding Students Regarding Personal-Social Problems.

To what extent

1. are students helped to analyze their social, emotional and personal problems?......

ITEM	Extent of Use Check (√) One				
	Not at all	Little	Some	Great	Very Great
2. is time available for conferences with a counselor on these problems?...............					
3. are definite procedures followed for helping students solve their personal-social problems?					
c. The Counseling Process. To what extent does the guidance program provide the student with opportunities for individual counseling which will help him to					
1. appraise his assets and liabilities?					
2. understand relationships between his assets and liabilities and his responsibilities and opportunities?					
3. plan a program of action?					
4. put the plan into effect?....					
5. make adjustments to changing conditions?					
d. Counseling the High School Student Regarding Educational Plans. To what extent does the guidance program assist each student to					
1. match his capacities with school opportunities?					
2. orient himself to the school?					

ITEM	Extent of Use Check (V) One				
	Not at all	Little	Some	Great	Very Great
3. plan his program with reference to required and elective subjects?					
4. secure accurate information on graduation requirements?					
5. secure accurate information regarding further educational opportunities?					
6. secure accurate information regarding college entrance requirements?					
7. improve his study habits?....					
e. Counseling the High School Student Regarding Vocational Plans.					
To what extent does the guidance program assist the student to					
1. appraise his abilities?					
2. secure information about occupational opportunities?					
3. match his personal assets with the requirements of vocational opportunities?					
4. plan for training, placement and growth on the job?....					
5. maintain a contact with his school after graduation by means of follow-up reports, etc.?					

ITEM	Extent of Use Check (√) One				
	Not at all	Little	Some	Great	Very Great
VI. Provision of Modern Guidance Material.					
See Chapter VI for a discussion of modern guidance materials.					
To what extent					
a. are books and supplementary materials appropriate to all levels of student ability used by the school?..............................					
b. are audio-visual aids in guidance used by the school?.........					
c. are sources of information about jobs available to students and faculty?......................					
d. are basic reference books for guidance workers used by the faculty?					
VII. Techniques for Promoting Professional Growth in Guidance Activies.					
See Chapter VII for a discussion of techniques for promoting professional growth in guidance activities.					
To what extent					
a. are opportunities to participate in a program of in-service education available to all members of the staff?................					
b. is the program of in-service education continuous, cooperative, challenging to all?..........					

ITEM	Extent of Use Check (√) One				
	Not at all	Little	Some	Great	Very Great
VIII. Techniques for Interpreting the Guidance Program. See Chapter VIII for discussion of techniques for interpreting the guidance program.					
To what extent					
a. is the guidance program interpreted to students? (by means of school paper, yearbook, bulletins, etc.)					
b. to school personnel? (by means of faculty meetings, committee meetings, etc.)					
c. to parents? (by means of conferences with teachers, counselors, principal, participation in parent-education groups, etc.).........................					
d. to the community? (through membership of school people in service clubs, activity in church groups, etc.).........					
e. is interpretation of guidance recognized as a two-way process—					
1. **to** students and **by** them to parents and community?....					
2. **to** school personnel and **by** them to students, parents?..					
3. **to** parents and **by** them to sons and daughters, other members of the community?					

| ITEM | Extent of Use   Check (V) One |||||
	Not at all	Little	Some	Great	Very Great
IX. Appraisal of the Guidance Program. To what extent a. do administrator and staff endeavor to appraise the effectiveness of the guidance program in meeting the needs of students?					
b. is the appraisal cooperative, comprehensive, continuous, student-centered, economical?					
c. is the program being modified in terms of the evaluation?....					

Suggestions for Evaluating the Educational Program.

Evaluation can be defined as the process of determining the effectiveness of the educational program in meeting the needs of boys and girls in a particular class, school and community. It involves collecting, summarizing and interpreting evidence of the extent to which educational objectives are being attained.

Basic Processes.

Certain processes are basic in all evaluation. These include the **formulation of definite objectives or purposes.** To be effective and functional, objectives need to be developed cooperatively by those who use them—teachers, administrators, students and parents. An **analysis of the objectives in terms of the behaviors involved** must then be made. Defined behaviorally, both teachers and students know exactly what the objective is and can observe and evaluate the behaviors indicated. A student who is developing good work habits;[1] for example, follows directions specificially and intelligently; works independently; is resourceful; concentrates on the job at hand; develops such habits as neatness, accuracy, promptness; is responsible regarding his obligations; selects wisely and makes proper use of books, materials and tools; participates consistently in group activities; knows when and how to seek help; observes critically; listens attentively and comprehends accurately what he hears.

A third basic process in evaluation is the **selection and provision of experiences** and **situations which will assist the student to achieve the types of behavior involved in the objective.** If the objective were "The student spells correctly the words he needs in his written work," many situations involving writing would need to be offered not only in English classes but in other classes as well.

The **selection or development of procedures for the collection of data** is the fourth basic process. For the more tangible objectives such as correct spelling, accuracy in mathematics, speed and comprehension in reading, the means of collecting evidence are readily available and easy to use. For less tangible objectives, such as work habits, the best technique is probably teacher observation.

Finally, the data must be **summarized** and **interpreted** if it is to be useful in diagnosing student needs or appraising progress. Usually this is best accomplished by translating all the data collected into a descriptive picture of the student's behavior, his successes in one area as seen against his difficulties and failures in another.

---

[1] Statement of Basic Objectives, Burbank Unified School District, Burbank, California, September, 1943.

COMPLETE

206 GUIDANCE HANDBOOK FOR SECONDARY SCHOOLS

Purpose

Characteristics of Evaluation. 2/

Evaluation is not new. Successful teachers and administrators have always endeavored to judge how effectively they were achieving their goals. It involves the strengthening and furthering of activities already under way rather than initiating new activities. But **evaluation must be comprehensive** and concerned with all aspects of the growth of the student, not with his intellectual growth alone. Of equal importance will be the student's growth and development in social behavior, health, interests, attitudes, work habits, study skills, use of leisure time, etc. **It is also a continuous process** and not just an end-point of the year's work. Even more important than the final test is the diagnosis of student and class needs at the beginning of the year, with an appropriate selection of testing, observational and recording activities throughout the year.

Teachers, administrators, students and parents should all be involved at different levels of participation in the formulation and definition of objectives, and in the collection and interpretation of evidence. Thus **evaluation is a cooperative enterprise.** It is obvious that more growth will take place if students participate in setting up objectives so that they know clearly the goals toward which they are working, and also the purpose of each educational experience in relation to these goals. The reaction of parents to school objectives and procedures can be especially helpful in the evaluative process.

Evaluation emphasizes growth and is concerned primarily with appraising the progress which a student has made in terms of his needs and interests and not merely with measuring his status in the group or the status of the group, the school or the program in relation to a national norm. Nor is evaluation a "program" in itself. Rather it is an integral phase of the educational program of the school and is **allied with all that goes on in the classroom and in the school.**

Evidence regarding the student's attainment of some objectives must be collected by description in addition to or in place of measurement. Growth in ability to cooperate, to exercise self-control, to respect rules and regulations, to be tolerant, can best be revealed by means of descriptive statements of significant behavior rather than by a score. Hence **evaluation is descriptive as well as quantitative.**

Evaluation is a long-term process. It involves study over many years of the effectiveness of the educational program in meeting its goals, and a revision of objectives, curricular experiences and approved techniques in accordance with the findings, and **it must be cumulative** since a major function of evaluation is to reveal a student's growth in the basic objectives.

Finally, if teachers are to accept evaluation and use its techniques, **it must also be economical.** Every justifiable shortcut should be taken to reduce and simplify the evaluative activities of the teacher. Wherever possible, scoring of tests should be performed by mechanical devices. Records for accumulating data should involve a minimum of clerical work. Test results for individual students should be presented by means of profiles, charts and other devices which will simplify their interpretation. Periodically an analysis should be made of the materials and techniques involved in the basic processes of evaluation in order to secure greater simplicity, clarity and economy.

Description Research and 23

Techniques of Evaluation.

There are many techniques available to teachers for collecting data regarding student growth and development. The teacher should select and use those which will be most appropriate in terms of the needs of her class and in terms of her own time and energy. **Standardized tests of skills and knowledge** are an essential phase of any evaluation program.

The tests which are given should fit in with basic objectives and be so integrated with the instructional program that remedial and corrective materials will be available for use with individual students and entire classes.

Tests, however, should not constitute the entire or even the major part of the evaluation process. Other techniques such as the **case study** and **interview** have been described in Chapter II. The **anecdotal record** is one of the most valuable of several techniques useful in gathering and recording significant data not amenable to testing. The method involves the recording by the teacher of specific student behavior which is indicative of success or failure in achieving an objective. Such records should be impersonal, clear, brief, revealing and indicative of general trends in the student's behavior. **Autobiographies and student questionnaires** are valuable in diagnosing problems of personal and social adjustment as well as determining academic, vocational and recreational plans for the future. Likewise **interest and adjustment inventories,** and **rating scales,** although such instruments have readily recognizable limitations, can, when cautiously used, secure information regarding students' school and vocational interests and personal-social adjustment which is of value to teacher and student. **Sociometric techniques** either of the type in which individuals choose others with whom they would or would not like to be associated, or the reputation or "guess who" test, assist teachers in discovering the underlying psychological structure of their classroom and to become more conscious of the need for friendship and for personal and social adjustment on the part of students in the class.

Samples of students' work, such as themes and reports, records of books read, summaries of leisure time activities, samples of poems, drawings, and construction work, all afford additional evidence of a student's growth in relation to basic educational objectives.

Services of Evaluation.

As an integral, dynamic process in modern education, evaluation assists schools: (1) in making a periodic check on the effectiveness of the educational institution, and thus indicating the points at which improvements in the program are necessary; (2) in validating the hypotheses upon which the educational institution operates; (3) in providing a psychological security to the school staff, to the students and to the parents; (4) in developing a sound basis for public relations; and (5) in providing information basic to effective guidance of individual students.[2]

---

[2] Eugene R. Smith, and Ralph W. Tyler, *Appraising and Recording Student Progress.* New York: Harper and Brothers, Pp. 4-11.

SELECTED REFERENCES

A. BOOKS

Allen, Wendell C., *Cumulative Pupil Records.*
New York: Teachers College,
Columbia University, 1943.

Bell, Howard M., *Matching Youth and Jobs.*
Washington 6, D. C.:
American Council on Education, 1940.

Bennett, Margaret E., and Hand, Harold C., *School and Life.*
Group Guidance Series, Vol. I;
New York: McGraw-Hill Book Company, 1938.

———————————, *Design for Personality.*
Group Guidance Series, Vol. II;
New York: McGraw-Hill Book Company, 1938.

———————————, *Beyond High School.*
Group Guidance Series, Vol. III;
New York: McGraw-Hill Book Company, 1938.

Bingham, Walter V., *Aptitudes and Aptitude Testing.*
New York: Harper and Brothers, 1937.

———————————, and Moore, Bruce V., *How to Interview.*
New York: Harper and Brothers, 1941.

Brainard, Paul P., *What About Yourself?*
Los Angeles: H. H. McClure Publishing Company, 1939.

Brewer, John M., et al., *History of Vocational Guidance.*
New York: Harper and Brothers, 1942.

Brown, Howard E., *Your Life in a Democracy.*
Chicago: J. B. Lippincott and Company, 1944.

Buros, Oscar, *The 1940 Mental Measurements Yearbook.*
Highland Park, New Jersey:
The Mental Measurements Yearbook, 1941.

Chisholm, Leslie L., *Guiding Youth in the Secondary School.*
San Francisco: American Book Company, 1945.

Cobb, Stanley, *Borderlands of Psychiatry.*
Cambridge, Massachusetts:
Harvard University Press, 1943.

Cox, W. L., and Duff, John C., *Guidance by the Classroom Teacher.*
New York: Prentice-Hall, Inc., 1941.

Crawford, C. C., et al., *Living Your Life.*
New York: D. C. Heath and Company, 1940.

Crow, Lester D., and Crow, Alice, *Mental Hygiene in School and Home Life.*
New York: McGraw-Hill Book Company, 1942.

Darley, John, *Testing and Counseling in the High School Guidance Program.*
Chicago: Science Research Associates, 1943.

Driscoll, Gertrude, *How to Observe the Behavior of Children.*
New York: Teachers College, Columbia University, 1936.

Dunbar, H. Flanders, new edition, *Emotions and Bodily Changes.*
New York: Columbia University Press, 1939.

Dunsmoor, C. C., and Miller, L. M., *Guidance Methods for Teachers.*
Scranton: International Book Company, 1942.

Edmonson, J. B., et al., *The Administration of the Modern Secondary School.*
New York: The Macmillan Company, 1941.

Eichler, Lillian, *The New Etiquette.*
New York: Garden City Publishing Company, 1939.

Fenton, Norman, *Mental Hygiene in School Practice.*
Palo Alto, California: Stanford University Press, 1944.

Fine, Benjamin, *School Publicity.*
New York: Harper and Brothers, 1943.

Folsom, Joseph K., *Plan for Marriage.*
New York: Harper and Brothers, 1938.

Forrester, Gertrude, *Methods of Vocational Guidance.*
Boston: D. C. Heath and Company, 1944.

Gates, Arthur I., et al., *Educational Psychology.*
New York: The Macmillan Company, 1942.

Germane, Charles E., and Germane, Edith G., *Personnel Work in High School.*
Chicago: Silver Burdett Company, 1941.

Goldstein, Sydney E., *Marriage and Family Counseling.*
New York: McGraw-Hill Book Company, 1941.

Goodrich, Laurence B., *Living With Others.*
San Francisco: American Book Company, 1939.

Grinnell, J. Earle, *Interpreting the Public Schools*.
New York: McGraw-Hill Book Company ,1937.

Hamrin, Shirley A., and Erickson, C. E., *Guidance in the Secondary School*.
New York: D. Appleton-Century Company, 1939.

Harap, Henry. et al., *The Changing Curriculum*.
New York: D. Appleton-Century Company, 1939.

Johnson, B. Lamar, editor, *General Education in the American High School*.
Chicago: Scott, Foresman and Company, 1942.

Jones, Arthur J., *Principles of Guidance*.
New York: McGraw-Hill Book Company, 1945.

Kefauver, Grayson N., and Hand, Harold C., *Appraising Guidance in Secondary Schools*.
New York: Macmillan Company, 1941.

Koos, Leonard V., et al., *Administering the Secondary School*.
San Francisco: American Book Company, 1940.

Landis, Paul H., and Landis, Judson T., *Social Living*.
San Francisco: Ginn and Company, 1938.

Lee, J. Murray, *A Guide to Measurement in Secondary Schools*.
New York: D. Appleton-Century Company, 1936.

Lefever, D. Welty, et al., *Principles and Techniques of Guidance*.
New York: The Ronald Press Company, 1941.

Leonard, Margaret L., *Health Counseling for Girls*.
New York: A. S. Barnes and Company, 1944.

Lloyd-Jones, Esther, and Fedder, Ruth, *Coming of Age*.
New York: McGraw-Hill Book Company, 1941.

McCall, William, *Measurement*.
New York: The Macmillan Company, 1938.

Moehlman, Arthur B., *School Administration*.
Boston: Houghton-Mifflin Company, 1940.

Murray, Elwood, *The Speech Personality*.
Chicago: J. B. Lippincott and Company, 1946.

Myers, George E., *Principles and Techniques of Vocational Guidance*.
New York: McGraw-Hill Book Company, 1941.

Nash, J. B., *Teachable Moments*.
New York: A. S. Barnes and Company, 1938.

Paterson, Donald C., et al., *Student Guidance Techniques*.
New York: McGraw-Hill Book Company, 1938.

Prescott, Daniel A., *Emotion and the Educative Process.*
Washington, D. C.: American Council on Education, 1938.

Reed, Anna Y., *Guidance and Personnel Services in Education.*
Ithaca, New York: Cornell University Press, 1944.

Remmers, H. H., and Gage, N. L., *Educational Measurement and Evaluation.*
New York: Harper and Brothers, 1943.

Rogers, Carl R., *Counseling and Psychotherapy.*
Boston: Houghton-Miffiin Company, 1942.

_____, and Wallen, J. L., *Counseling with Returned Servicemen.*
New York: McGraw-Hill Book Company, 1946.

Smith, Charles M., and Roos, Mary M., *Guide to Guidance.*
New York: Prentice-Hall, Inc., 1942.

Smith, E. R., and Tyler, R. W., *Appraising and Recording Student Progress.*
New York: Harper and Brothers, 1943.

Strang, Ruth, *Every Teacher's Records.*
New York: Teachers College, Columbia University, 1936.

_____, *Pupil Personnel and Guidance.*
New York: The Macmillan Company, 1940.

_____, et al., *Gateways to Readable Books.*
New York: H. W. Wilson Company, 1944.

Super, Donald E., *Dynamics of Vocational Adjustment.*
New York: Harper and Brothers, 1942.

Thorpe, Louis P., *Child Psychology and Development.*
New York: The Ronald Press Company, 1946.

_____, *Psychological Foundations of Personality.*
New York: McGraw-Hill Book Company, 1938.

Tiegs, Ernest W., and Katz, Barney, *Mental Hygiene in Education.*
New York: Ronald Press Company, 1941.

Traxler, Arthur E., *Techniques of Guidance.*
New York: Harper and Brothers, 1945.

Troyer, Maurice E., and Pace, C. Robert, *Evaluation in Teacher Education.*
Washington, D. C.: American Council on Education, 1944.

Tyler, Harry E., et al., *Learning to Live.*
New York: Farrar and Rinehart, 1940.

Uhl, Willis L., and Powers, Francis E., *Personal and Social Adjustment.*
New York: The Macmillan Company, 1938.

Williamson, E. G., *How to Counsel Students*.
New York: McGraw-Hill Book Company, 1939.

———————————, and Darley, J. E., *Student Personnel Work*.
New York: McGraw-Hill Book Company, 1937.

———————————, and Hahn, M. E., *Introduction to High School Counseling*.
New York: McGraw-Hill Book Company, 1940.

Woodworth, Robert S., *Psychology*.
New York: Henry Holt and Company, 1940.

B. LOS ANGELES COUNTY SUPERINTENDENT OF SCHOOLS PUBLICATIONS

Clark, Willis W., "Observation in Education."
Bulletin No. 9013; Los Angeles 12: Division of Research and Guidance, 1940.

"Listen."
Monthly Radio Bulletin; Los Angeles 12: Division of Audio-Visual Education.

Nolan, Esther Grace, "How May Secondary Teachers Distinguish Between a Case of Severe Reading Difficulty and One of Low Mental Development?" Bulletin No. 9049; Los Angeles 12: Division of Research and Guidance, May, 1942.

Occupational Information, Revised. A Bibliography of Books, Pamphlets, Periodicals and Film Titles.
Monograph No. 16005; Los Angeles 12: Division of Research and Guidance, Sept., 1947.

"Pleasure-Reading Books for Slow-Learning Groups at the Junior and Senior High School Level."
Bulletin E-18; Los Angeles 12: Division of Secondary Education, September, 1941.

"Statement of Elementary School Promotion Policy."
Bulletin No. 8103; Los Angeles 12: Division of Research and Guidance, 1940.

"Suggested Functions, Qualifications and Preparation of Guidance Personnel."
Bulletin No. 15000; Los Angeles 12: Division of Research and Guidance, July, 1946.

"Textbooks and Instructional Materials Evaluated."
Bulletin No. 6169; Los Angeles 12: Division of Research and Guidance, 1938.

"Textbooks and Instructional Materials Evaluated."
Bulletin No. 7130; Los Angeles 12: Division of Research and Guidance, April, 1939.

"Textbooks and Instructional Material Evaluated." Bulletin No. 8010;
Los Angeles 12: Division of Research and Guidance, August, 1939.

"The Reading Process."
Bulletin No. 8093; Los Angeles 12: Division of Research and Guidance, May, 1940.

"Visual Aids Catalog for Junior and Senior High Schools."
Bulletin Special, No. 22; Los Angeles 12: Division of Audio-Visual Education, September, 1943.

"Supplement to Visual Aids Catalog for Junior and Senior High Schools."
Bulletin Special, No. 12: 4-5; Los Angeles 12: Division of Audio-Visual Education, September, 1944.

"1945 Catalog of Sponsored Visual Aids for Elementary and Secondary Schools."
Bulletin Special, No. 67: 4-5; Los Angeles 12: Division of Audio-Visual Education, January, 1945.

"Supplement to Visual Aids Catalog for Junior and Senior High Schools."
Bulletin Special, No. 98: 5-6; Los Angeles 12: Division of Audio-Visual Education, May, 1946.

C. PERIODICAL ARTICLES

Hershey, John O., "A Mobile Occupational Library in the Classroom,"
Occupations, 24: 91, November, 1945.

Nolan, Esther Grace, "Reading Difficulty Versus Low Mentality," *California Journal of Secondary Education*, 17: 34-39, January, 1942.

_____, "Training Teachers to Use Measurement as a Guidance Tool," *Education*, 66: 436-442, March, 1946.

Occupations. Vocational Guidance Journal; New York: National Vocational Guidance Association.

"Public Relations Number," *Education*, Volume 66, No. 10, June, 1946.

"Pupil Guidance in the Classroom," *Los Angeles School Journal*, Vol. XXI, No. 29, April 25, 1938.

Rogers, Carl R., "Significant Aspects of Client-Centered Therapy," *The American Psychologist*, I: 10, October, 1946.

"Secondary Schools and the Community," *California Journal of Secondary Education*, Vol. 21, No. 6, December 15, 1946.

Sheviakov, George, "'The Necessity of Understanding the Adolescent as a Basis for Curriculum and Guidance," *Journal of the National Association of Deans of Women*, 5: 7-12, October, 1941.

"Supplement to Pupil Guidance in the Classroom," *Los Angeles School Journal*, Vol. XXIII, No. 29, April 29, 1940.

Thorne, F. C., "A Critique of Non-Directive Methods of Psychotherapy," *Journal of Abnormal and Social Psychology*, 39: 459-470, 1944.

——————, "Directive Psychotherapy," *Journal of Clinical Psychology*, 2: 68-79, 1946.

Traxler, Arthur E., "Cumulative Test Records: Their Nature and Uses," *Educational and Psychological Measurement*, I: 323-340, October, 1941.

D. SPECIAL MATERIALS

American Job Series of Occupational Monographs.
    Chicago 4: Science Research Associates, 228 South Wabash Avenue.

California Cumulative Guidance Record for Elementary Schools.
    San Francisco 8: A. Carlisle and Company, 135 Post St.

California Cumulative Record, Junior and Senior High Schools.
    Long Beach, California: Dr. Harold B. Brooks, Long Beach Public Schools.

California State Reconstruction and Reemployment Commission, "Postwar Objectives of Public Education in California." Unpublished report, The Commission, Sacramento 14, February, 1945.

Career—Research Monographs.
    Chicago 5: Institute of Research, 537 South Dearborn St.

Commonwealth Vocational Guidance Monographs.
    Chicago 4: Commonwealth Book Company, 80 East Jackson Boulevard.

Free and Near—Free Occupational Material.
    Lincoln, Nebraska: State Board of Vocational Education.

Guideposts to Occupational Information.
    Port Byron, New York: Chronicle Publishing Company.

Occupational Abstracts.
New York City 3: Occupational Index, Inc., New York University, Washington Square.

Occupational Briefs.
Port Byron, New York: New York State Department of Education, Guidance Bureau.

Occupational Briefs.
Chicago 4: Science Research Associates, 228 South Wabash Avenue.

Occupational Briefs.
Pasadena 1, California: Western Personnel Service, 130 Raymond Avenue.

Occupational Reprints.
Chicago 4: Science Research Associates, 228 South Wabash Avenue.

Success Vocational Information Monographs.
Chicago 40: Morgan-Dillon and Company, 4616 North Clark Street.

Thorpe, Louis P., and Clark, Willis W., *Manual of Directions, Mental Health Analysis*, Secondary Series.
Los Angeles: California Test Bureau, 1946.

Vocational Guidance Manuals.
New York City 19: Vocational Guidance Manuals, Inc., 45 West 45th Street.

Vocational Guidance Series.
Rochester 8, New York: Rochester Institute of Technology.

Vocational Monographs.
Chicago 1: Quarrie Corporation, 35 East Wacker Drive.

Vocational—Professional Monographs.
Boston 8: Bellman Publishing Company, 6 Park Street.

Vocations for Women.
New York City 23: National Federation of Business and Professional Women's Clubs, Inc., 1819 Broadway.

Way of Life Series.
Evanston, Illinois: Row, Peterson and Cnmpany.

Your Future Series.
Baltimore: Baltimore Department of Education, Division of Vocational Education.

E. UNITED STATES GOVERNMENT PUBLICATIONS

Census Bureau Publications.
 Bureau of Census; Washington 25, D. C.: Superintendent of Documents.

Descriptions of Professions Series.
 Washington 25, D. C.: National Roster of Scientific and Specialized Personnel, via Superintendent of Documents.

Dictionary of Occupational Titles and Codes, Parts I to IV and Supplements.
 Washington 25, D. C.: United States Employment Service, via Superintendent of Documents.

Guidance Leaflets.
 Washington 25, D. C.: U. S. Office of Education, via Superintendent of Documents.

Handbooks of Descriptions of Specialized Fields.
 Washington 25, D. C.: National Roster of Scientific and Specialized Personnel, via Superintendent of Documents.

Individual Inventory in Guidance Programs in Secondary Schools.
 United States Office of Education, Vocational Division, Bulletin No. 215; Washington, D. C.: Superintendent of Documents, 1941.

Individual Job Descriptions.
 Washington 25, D. C.: U. S. Department of Labor, via Superintendent of Documents.

Industrial Job Family Set.
 Washington 25, D. C.: U. S. War Manpower Commission.

Industrial Series.
 Washington 25, D. C.: U. S. Department of Commerce, via Superintendent of Documents.

Industry Series: Labor Market Information for USES Counselling.
 Washington 25, D. C.: U. S. Department of Labor, 1945.

Labor Market Area Statements.
 Washington 25, D. C.: U. S. War Manpower Commission.

Labor Market Monthly.
 Washington 25, D. C.: U. S. War Manpower Commission.

Occupation Job Family Set.
 Washington 25, D. C.: U. S. War Manpower Commission.

Occupational Briefs.
 Washington 25, D. C.: National Roster of Scientific and Specialized Personnel, via Superintendent of Documents.

Occupational Briefs.
Washington 25, D. C.: U. S. War Department, via Superintendent of Documents.

Occupational Information and Guidance Series.
United States Office of Education; Washington 25, D. C.: Superintendent of Documents.

Occupational Outlook Division Series.
Washington 25, D. C.: U. S. Department of Labor, via Superintendent of Documents.

Outlook for Women in Occupations in Medical Services.
Washington 25, D. C.: U. S. Department of Labor, via Superintenden of Documents.

Ruch, G. M., and Segel, David, *Minimum Essentials of the Individual Inventory in Guidance.*
United States Office of Education, Vocational Division, Bulletin No. 202; Washington, D. C.: Superintendent of Documents, 1938.

Segel, David, *Nature and Use of the Cumulative Record.*
United States Office of Education, Bulletin No. 3; Washington, D. C.: Superintendent of Documents, 1938.

Vocational Monographs.
Washington 25, D. C.: U. S. War Manpower Commission.

F. YEARBOOKS AND MONOGRAPHS

Bacher, O. R., and Berkowitz, G, J., *School Courses and Related Careers.*
Chicago: Science Research Associates, 1945.

California State Department of Education, *List of High School Textbooks.*
Bulletin, Vol. XVI, No. 2; Sacramento: Library and Courts Building, August, 1947.

California State Department of Education, *Vocational Education in California.*
Bulletin XIV, No. 4; Sacramento: Bureau of Vocational Education, October, 1945.

California State Reconstruction and Reemployment Commission, *How Many Jobs for Californians?*
Sacramento 14: The Commission, 1944.

Clark, Edwin L., *Petting—Wise or Otherwise?*
New York: Association Press, 1939.

Cole, Luella, and Ferguson, Jessie M., *Students' Guide to Efficient Study*.
New York: Farrar and Rinehart, 1935.

Commission on Teacher Education, *Helping Teachers Understand Children*.
Division on Child Development and Teacher Personnel; Washington, D. C.: American Council on Education, 1945.

Commission on Teacher Education, "Physiological Aspects of Child Growth and Development."
Division on Child Development and Teacher Personnel; Washington, D. C.: American Council on Education, June, 1941.

Educational Policies Commission, *Education for All American Youth*.
Washington, D. C.: National Education Association ,1944.

Educational Policies Commission, *The Purpose of Education in American Democracy*.
Washington, D. C.: National Education Association, 1938.

Ellingson, Mark, and Jarvie, L. I., *Handbook on the Anecdotal Behavior Journal*.
Chicago: University of Chicago Bookstore, 1940.

Group Planning in Education.
1945 Yearbook, Department of Supervision and Curriculum Development; Washington 6, D. C.: National Education Association, 1945.

Head, Gay, *Boy Dates Girl*.
New York: Scholastic Corporation, 1937.

Health Education.
Report of Joint Committee on Health Problems in Education; Washington, D. C.: National Education Association, 1941.

Health in Schools.
Twentieth Yearbook, American Association of School Administrators; Washington, D. C.; The Association, 1942.

Los Angeles City Superintendent of Schools, *Books Evaluated by Means of the Vocabulary Grade Placement Formula*.
Los Angeles 12: Los Angeles City Schools, March, 1937.

_____, *The Improvement of Reading in Secondary Schools*.
School Publication No. 358; Los Angeles 12: Los Angeles City Schools, 1940.

_____, *Guidance in Elementary Schools*. School Publication No. 398; Los Angeles 12: Los Angeles City Schools, 1944.

Mackenzie, Gordon H., "Implications for Teachers and Counselors," *Forty-Third Yearbook of the National Society for the Study of Education*, Part I, Chicago: University of Chicago Bookstore, 1944.

Meek (Stolz), Lois H., et al., *Personal-Social Development of Boys and Girls*.
New York: Progressive Education Association, 1940.

Mental Health in the Classroom.
Thirteenth Yearbook, Department of Supervisors and Directors of Instruction; Washington 6, D. C.: National Education Association, 1941.

Schmaelzle, O. I., editor, *A Guide to Counseling*.
San Francisco: San Francisco Public Schools, 1944.

Schools in Small Communities.
Seventeenth Yearbook, American Association of School Administrators; Washington, D. C.: The Association, 1939.

Smith, Samuel, and Littlefield, Arthur W., *Best Methods of Study*.
New York: Barnes and Noble, Inc., 1938.

Tryon, Caroline, *Evaluation of Adolescent Personality by Adolescents*.
Society for Research in Child Development; Washington, D. C.: National Research Council, 1940.

University of the State of New York, *Pupil Progress in Elementary Schools of New York State*.
Bulletin No. 1297; Albany: New York State Department of Education, July, 1945.

Webster, B. C., *Guidance for the High School Pupil*.
Montreal: McGill University Press, 1940.

Yale, John R., editor, *Frontier Thinking in Guidance*.
Chicago: Science Research Associates, 1945.

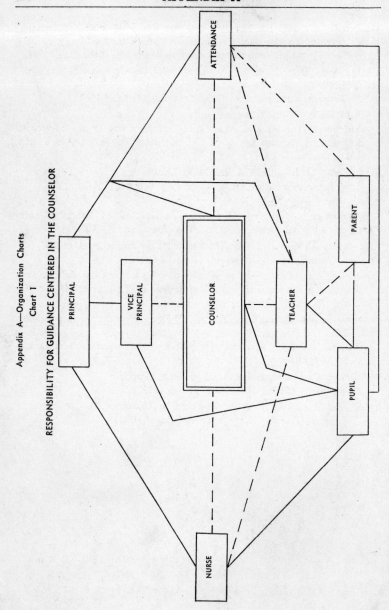

Appendix A—Organization Charts
Chart 1

RESPONSIBILITY FOR GUIDANCE CENTERED IN THE COUNSELOR

Appendix A—Organization Charts
Chart 2

RESPONSIBILITY FOR GUIDANCE CENTERED IN THE TEACHER

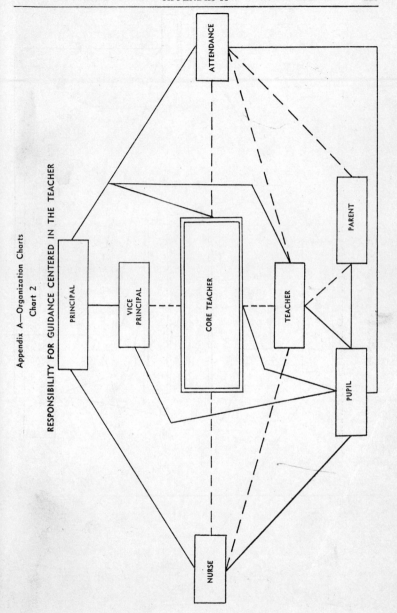

Appendix A—Organization Charts
Chart 3

RESPONSIBILITY FOR GUIDANCE CENTERED IN THE DIRECTOR OF GUIDANCE

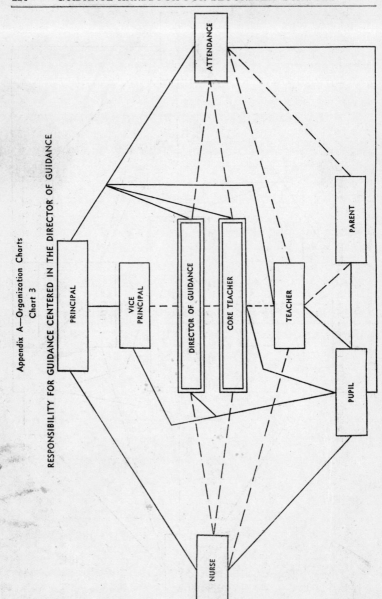

APPENDIX B

STRENGTHENING OBJECTIVE TESTING PROCEDURES

Careful adherence to the suggestions which follow will enable the Division of Research and Guidance to provide a more prompt and accurate service.

Many of the suggestions listed are already being practiced by teachers, counselors and testing supervisors. However, attention to those details that are not being practiced will constitute a definite contribution to the effectiveness of the testing program of the district as well as to the service provided by the Division of Research and Guidance.

Suggestions for Strengthening Objective Testing Procedures

I. **Preliminaries.**

These items need attention before giving the test:

A. The best possible provision for lighting.

B. Adequate ventilation.

C. Seating arranged to enable students to work independently.

D. The distribution and collection of materials.

E. A check on the correct edition, battery and form of the test.

F. A check, when machine-scoring tests are used, to verify the matching of answer sheets with the test booklet as to edition, battery and form.

G. A check on the proper type of machine-scoring pencil for marking the answer sheets.

H. Plans made to test according to standardized procedures:

    1. Effort to make the testing situation approach that of the normal classroom as closely as possible.

    2. Effort to group students for testing in small rather than large groups.

    3. Effort to avoid testing immediately before or after the lunch period.

I. Provision of a watch with a second hand when required.

II. Giving the Tests.

These items need attention before and during the test:

A. Study and practice of the test directions by the examiner.

B. Demonstration of the proper method of using the answer sheet for machine-scoring tests.

C. Helping the students to do their best on the test by:

    1. Establishing and maintaining calm, quiet working conditions.

    2. Checking on close attention to work.

    3. Giving clearly enunciated and exact directions.

D. Accurate timing of the test sections.

E. A record made on the test booklet or answer page to indicate that a student had done any of the following:

    1. Copied from another pupil's paper.

    2. Worked on the wrong page.

    3. Had lost time because of a broken or empty pencil.

    4. Marked the booklet or answer page incorrectly.

5. Had been handicapped by deficient vision or hearing.

6. Indicated disinterest through poor posture or attitude.

7. Had been handicapped by fatigue.

8. Was emotionally upset by the testing situation.

9. Other situations.

III. Clerical Details.

These items need attention during and after the test:

A. Check the accuracy of the information supplied by the student on the test booklet or answer sheet:

   1. Full name of student printed or written legibly.

   2. Correct identification of the student as to:

      a. School.

      b. Grade (Example: 7A or 4B).

      c. Teacher.

      d. Sex.

      e. Age at time of testing (months preferable but years and months acceptable).

      f. Birth dates, when called for, should be given as month, day and year.

B. Verify the above information when such is necessary.

   1. Check the date of birth of the student with the class register.

C. Points to observe in hand-scoring:

   1. Check the test and answer keys to insure that they correspond as to edition, battery and form.

   2. A colored pencil should be used for marking.

   3. Test items should be marked so that correct and incorrect items are distinguished.

D. Points to observe in machine-scoring:

1. Check the answer pages of machine-scoring tests for correct marking and the removal of extraneous marks.

2. One and only one response should be made for each question. Otherwise, the answer page cannot be scored. Scan papers and erase items having more than one response.

3. Each response should be indicated with a solid black pencil mark between the small dotted lines —not crosses or checks. Otherwise, the machine will not properly record the answers.

4. The old marks should be completely erased in questions involving a change of response.

5. All stray marks on or near the answer spaces should be erased.

6. The answer pages should be handled carefully; they should not be creased, folded or clipped when in use or when shipped to the County Office.

7. Hand-scored sections of machine-scoring tests should be correctly marked **before** shipment to the County Office.

E. All machine-scoring pencils and test materials should be turned in to the examiner when testing is complete.

F. Materials sent to the County Office should be arranged alphabetically, by student, and grouped, by grade and teacher. Answer sheets for parts of tests such as arithmetic and language should be kept separate.

G. The Test Data Verification Sheet should be filled in properly and submitted with materials sent to the County for processing.

APPENDIX C

TEST DATA VERIFICATION SHEET

This verification sheet should be filled in completely by the teacher (for the classroom) and submitted with any testing materials, either hand or machine-scored, which are sent to the Division of Research and Guidance for processing. If a special examiner gives tests to several groups only one verification sheet need be submitted.

Please fill in each item. When more than one test is given at a sitting, the additional identifying data should be supplied.

Identifying data:

District.. School..

Grade............Teacher (or teachers)..

Achievement test: Name of test..

    Battery................Form................ Date administered......................

Intelligence test: Name of test..

    Battery................Form................ Date administered......................

Other test: Name of test..

    Battery................Form................ Date administered......................

The following data have been verified for each student:

School.

Grade (example: 7A or 9B).

Teacher.

Full name of student.

Sex.

Age at time of testing (months preferable but years and months acceptable).

Birthdates, when called for, should be given as month, day and year.

All hand-scored sections of machine-scoring tests have been accurately corrected before shipment.

The separate answer pages have been handled carefully and not folded, creased or clipped while in use or when shipped.

The materials have been arranged alphabetically by student and grouped by teacher and grade. Answer sheets for parts of tests such as arithmetic, language, etc. have been kept separate.

The bulletin entitled "Strengthening Objective Testing Procedures" has been used in connection with the above testing.

Remarks: (Please record special conditions which might cause errors of measurement.)

Signed...

Teacher (or Examiner)

LOS ANGELES COUNTY SUPERINTENDENT OF SCHOOLS
DIVISION OF RESEARCH AND GUIDANCE

Summary of Intelligence and Achievement

DISTRICT_____ BATTERY_____ FORM_____ DATE TESTED_____

SCHOOL_____ BATTERY_____ FORM_____ DATE TESTED_____

GRADE_____

TEACHER_____

TESTS USED:
INTELLIGENCE_____
ACHIEVEMENT_____

INTELLIGENCE QUOTIENT

	NON-LANGUAGE	LANGUAGE	TOTAL

	VERY SLOW LEARNING		SLOW LEARNING		AVERAGE		RAPID LEARNING		VERY RAPID LEARNING				NO. IN GRADE	AVERAGE		ACTUAL G.P.
	50 59	60 69	70 79	80 89	90 99	100 109	110 119	120 129	130 139	140 149	150 ABOVE					

GRADE PLACEMENT	5.9	6.0 6.4	6.5 6.9	7.0 7.4	7.5 7.9	8.0 8.4	8.5 8.9	9.0 9.4	9.5 9.9	10.0 10.4	10.5 10.9	11.0 11.4	11.5 11.9	12.0 12.4	12.5 12.9	13.0 13.4	13.5 13.9	14.0 14.4	14.5 14.9	15.0 15.4	15.5 15.9	16.0 +	PUPILS	AVE.	DEVIATIONS FROM ACT. G.P.	DEVIATIONS FROM M.A. G.P.
CHRONOLOGICAL AGE G.P.																										
MENTAL AGE G.P.																										
READING VOCABULARY																										
READING COMPREHENSION																										
TOTAL READING																										
ARITHMETIC REASONING																										
ARITHMETIC FUNDAMENTALS																										
TOTAL ARITHMETIC																										
LANGUAGE																										
SPELLING																										
TOTAL TEST G.P.																										

APPENDIX E

TESTS, INVENTORIES AND SCALES AVAILABLE
BY GRADE LEVELS

On the following pages may be found a list of tests, inventories and scales recommended for appraisal of pupil abilities and accomplishments in the secondary school. Administrators and teachers concerned with the provision of counseling and guidance facilities are encouraged to select appropriate tests and other instruments in consultation with the research and guidance coordinator assigned to the district.

Additional information regarding these and other evaluation instruments may be secured by consulting the Mental Measurements Yearbooks for 1938 and 1940, edited by Buros and published by Rutgers University.

PUBLISHING COMPANIES LISTED

A.P.N.Y.   Association Press, 347 Madison Avenue, New York.

C.T.B.   California Test Bureau, 5916 Hollywood Blvd., Los Angeles, Calif.

C.T.S.   Cooperative Test Service, 15 Amsterdam Avenue, New York.

E.T.B.   Educational Test Bureau, 720 Washington Ave., S. E., Minneapolis, Minn.

H.M.   Houghton-Mifflin Co., 2 Park St., Boston, Mass.; 612 Howard St., San Francisco.

McK.   McKnight and McKnight, Bloomington, Ill.

P.E.A.   Progressive Education Association, 6010 Dorches-
          ter Ave., Chicago, Ill.

P.C.   Psychological Corporation, 522 Fifth Ave., N. Y. 18.

P.S.P.C. Public School Publishing Company, Bloomington,
          Ill.

S.R.A.   Science Research Associates, 228 S. Wabash Ave.,
          Chicago 4, Ill.

S.U.I.   State University of Iowa, Iowa City, Iowa.

S.U.P.   Stanford University Press, Stanford University, Calif.

STO   C. H. Stoelting Co., Chicago, Ill.

T.C.   Teachers College, Columbia University, N. Y.

W.B.   World Book Company, Yonkers, N. Y.:   149 N
          Montgomery St., San Francisco.

I. Group Intelligence Tests

	7	8	9	10	11	12	13	14	HS	MS	PUBLISHER**
					GRADES				SCORING*		
American Council on Education Psychological Examination for High School Students.			X	X	X	X	X	X	X		CTS
California Test of Mental Maturity											
Intermediate Series	X	X	X	X	X	X	X	X	X	X	CTB
Advanced Series (Machine-scoring edition is known as California Intelligence Test)			X	X	X	X	X	X	X	X	
California Short-Form Test of Mental Maturity											CTB
Intermediate Short-Form	X	X	X	X	X				X	X	
Advanced Short-Form			X	X	X	X	X	X	X	X	
Chicago Test of Primary Mental Ability	X	X	X	X	X	X	X	X	X		SRA
Henmon-Nelson Test of Mental Ability	X	X	X	X	X	X			X		HM
Kuhlman-Anderson Intelligence Tests											ETB
Grades VII-VIII	X	X							X		
Grades IX to Maturity			X	X	X	X	X	X	X		

*Scoring: H.S.—hand-scored; M.S.—machine-scored.
**Publisher: See pages 232-233 for meaning of symbols.

	GRADES								SCORING		PUBLISHER
	7	8	9	10	11	12	13	14	HS	MS	
Ohio State University Psychological Test (Form 21)			X	X	X	X	X	X	X		SRA
Otis Group Intelligence Test Advanced Examination	X	X	X	X	X	X	X	X	X		WBC
Otis Quick-Scoring Mental Ability Tests											WBC
Beta Test	X	X	X						X	X	
Gamma Test			X	X	X	X	X	X	X	X	
Otis Self-Administering Test of Mental Ability			X	X	X	X	X	X	X		WBC
Intermediate Examination	X	X	X						X		
Higher Examination			X	X	X	X	X	X	X		
Pintner General Ability Tests											WBC
Intermediate Verbal	X	X	X						X	X	
Intermediate Non-Language	X	X	X						X	X	
Advanced			X	X	X	X	X	X	X	X	
Terman-McNemar Test of Mental Ability	X	X	X	X	X	X			X	X	WBC

II. Group Achievement Test Batteries

(Reading, Arithmetic and Language Combined)

	7	8	9	10	11	12	13	14	HS	MS	PUBLISHER
Iowa Every Pupil Tests of Basic Skills											
Advanced..............	x	x								x	HM
Metropolitan Achievement Tests											
Advanced..............	x	x							x		WBC
Progressive Achievement Test									x		CTB
Intermediate—Forms A, B, C........	x	x	x						x	x	
Advanced—Forms A, B, C........			x	x	x	x			x	x	
Progressive Tests in Social and Related Sciences	x	x							x	x	CTB
Stanford Achievement Test											
Advanced Battery..............	x	x	x						x	x	WBC

(GRADES: columns 7–14; SCORING: HS, MS)

III. Group Achievement Tests by Subject

Reading Tests

	7	8	9	10	11	12	13	14	HS	MS	PUBLISHER
Detroit Reading Test	X	X	X						X		WBC
Haggerty Reading Examination—Sigma 3	X	X	X	X	X	X			X		WBC
Ingraham-Clark Diagnostic Reading Intermediate	X	X								X	CTB
Diagnostic Examination of Silent Reading Abilities											ETB
Junior Division	X	X	X						X	X	
Senior Division				X	X	X			X	X	
Iowa Silent Reading Test											WBC
Elementary	X	X	X						X		
Advanced			X	X	X	X	X		X	X	
Metropolitan Reading Test	X	X							X		WBC
Progressive Reading Tests											CTB
Intermediate—Forms A. B. C.	X	X	X						X	X	
Advanced—Forms A. B. C.			X	X	X	X			X	X	
Sangren-Woody Reading Test Forms A and B	X	X	X						X		WBC
Stanford Achievement Tests Advanced Reading Test	X	X	X						X	X	WBC

	7	8	9	10	11	12	13	14	HS	MS	PUBLISHER
Arithmetic Tests											
Bruckner Diagnostic Arithmetic Tests											ETB
Whole Numbers	X	X							X		
Fractions	X	X							X		
Decimals	X	X							X		
Courtis Standard Practice Tests in Arithmetic	X	X							X		WBC
Metropolitan Arithmetic Test	X	X							X		WBC
Advanced	X	X							X		CTB
Progressive Arithmetic Test											
Intermediate—Forms A, B, C		X	X						X	X	
Advanced—Forms A, B, C			X	X	X	X			X	X	
Stanford Achievement Test											WBC
Advanced Arithmetic	X	X	X						X	X	
Language Tests											
Language Essentials Test	X	X							X		ETB
Progressive Language Tests											CTB
Intermediate	X	X	X						X	X	
Advanced			X	X	X	X			X	X	
Stanford Achievement Test											WBC
Advanced Language Arts	X	X	X						X	X	

Spelling

Use Spelling Section of any Achievement Battery

	7	8	9	10	11	12	13	14	HS	MS	PUBLISHER
Ayres Spelling Scale	X	X							X		SUI
Buckingham Extension of Ayres Scale	X	X							X		SUI
Iowa Spelling Scales	X	X							X		SUI
Morrison-McCall Spelling Scale	X	X							X		WBC
Wellesley Spelling Scale			X	X	X	X	X	X	X	X	CTB

Handwriting

Use Handwriting Section of any Achievement Battery

	7	8	9	10	11	12	13	14	HS	MS	PUBLISHER
Ayres Handwriting Scale									X		SUI
Freeman Chart for Diagnosing Faults in Handwriting									X		SUI
Gray Standard Score Card for Measuring Handwriting									X		SUI
Thorndike Handwriting Scale									X		SUI

		GRADES								SCORING		PUBLISHER
	7	8	9	10	11	12	13	14		HS	MS	
Armed Forces Institute Subject Tests— Form B. Cover wide variety of tests for high schools and colleges (Consult SRA catalog)			X	X	X	X	X	X		X	X	SRA
Iowa Tests of Educational Development— Forms X-1 and Y-1			X	X	X	X				X	X	SRA
Armed Forces Institute Tests of General Educational Development												SRA
Test No. 1 Correctness and Effectiveness of Expression			X	X	X	X	X	X		X	X	
Test No. 2 Interpretation of Reading Materials in the Social Studies			X	X	X	X	X	X		X	X	
Test No. 3 Interpretation of Reading Materials in the Natural Sciences			X	X	X	X	X	X		X	X	
Test No. 4 Interpretation of Literary Materials			X	X	X	X	X	X		X	X	
Test No. 5 General Mathematical Ability			X	X	X	X	X	X		X	X	

IV. Group Work and study Skill Tests.

	GRADES 7	8	9	10	11	12	13	14	SCORING HS	MS	PUBLISHER
Iowa Every Pupil Work-Study Skills (Advanced)	X	X								X	SUI
Interpretation of Data		X	X	X	X	X	X		X		PEA
Peabody Library Information Test			X	X	X	X	X		X		ETB
Library Test for Junior High Schools			X	X	X	X	X		X		CTB
Test on the Use of Books and Libraries			X	X					X		PEA
Tyler-Kimber Study Skills Test			X	X	X	X	X	X	X		SUP

V. Group Personal and Social Adjustment Inventories and Scales.

	GRADES 7	8	9	10	11	12	13	14	SCORING HS	MS	PUBLISHER
Baker, Telling What I Do	X	X	X						X		PSPC
Bell Adjustment Inventory	X	X	X	X	X	X	X	X	X		SUP
California Test of Personality											
Intermediate	X	X	X	X	X				X	X	CTB
Secondary			X	X	X	X	X	X	X	X	
Haggerty-Olson-Wickman Behavior Rating Schedule	X	X	X	X	X	X			X		WBC
Mental Health Analysis											
Intermediate	X	X	X	X	X				X	X	CTB
Secondary			X	X	X	X	X	X	X	X	
New York Rating Scale for School Habits	X	X	X	X	X	X	X		X		WBC
Rogers Test of Personality Adjustment	X	X	X	X	X	X			X		APNY
The Personal Audit			X	X	X	X	X	X	X		SRA
Washburn Social Adjustment Inventory	X	X	X	X	X	X			X	X	WBC

	GRADES								SCORING		PUBLISHER
	7	8	9	10	11	12	13	14	HS	MS	
VI. Group Interests Tests.											
Brainard Occupational Preference Inventory			X	X	X	X	X	X	X		PC
Interest Index	X	X	X	X	X	X			X		PEA
Kuder Preference Record			X	X	X	X	X	X	X	X	SRA
Occupational Interest Inventory											CTB
Intermediate	X	X	X	X					X	X	CTB
Advanced					X	X	X	X	X	X	SUP
Strong Vocational Interest Inventory					X	X	X	X	X	X	McK
Vocational Interest Inventory (Cleeton)			X	X	X	X	X	X	X		
VII. Group Health Tests.											
Neher Health Inventory for High School Students			X	X	X	X	X		X	X	CTB
VIII. Group Performance Tests.											
MacQuarrie Test for Mechanical Ability	X	X	X	X	X	X	X	X	X	X	CTB
Minnesota Paper Form Board	X	X	X	X	X	X	X		X	X	SRA
Prognostic Test of Mechanical Abilities	X	X	X	X	X	X	X	X	X	X	CTB
Stenquist Mechanical Aptitude Tests	X	X	X	X	X	X			X		WBC
Survey of Mechanical Insight			X	X	X	X	X	X	X	X	CTB
Survey of Object Visualization			X	X	X	X	X	X	X	X	CTB
Survey of Space Relations Ability			X	X	X	X	X	X	X	X	CTB
Survey of Working Speed and Accuracy			X	X	X	X	X	X	X	X	CTB

IX Individual Tests.

A. Intelligence

	7	8	9	10	11	12	13	14	HS	MS	PUBLISHER
Arthur Point Scale of Performance Tests	x	x	x	x	x	x			x		STO
Cornell-Coxe Performance Ability Scale.	x	x	x	x	x	x			x		WBC
Healy Picture Completion No. 2	x	x	x	x	x	x			x		STO
Stamford-Binet	x	x	x	x	x	x	x	x	x		H-M
Wechsler-Bellevue Intelligence Scale	x	x	x	x	x	x	x	x	x		PC

B. Reading

	7	8	9	10	11	12	13	14	HS	MS	PUBLISHER
Standardized Oral Reading Check Tests.	x	x							x		PSPC

C. Performance

	7	8	9	10	11	12	13	14	HS	MS	PUBLISHER
Minnesota Rate of Manipulation			x	x	x	x	x	x	x		ETB
Minnesota Spatial Relations Test			x	x	x	x	x	x	x		ETB
Pennsylvania Bi-Manual Worksample				x	x	x	x	x	x		ETB
Purdue Peg Board			x	x	x	x	x	x	x		SRA

This list of tests might well be extended to include other objective measures of special subjects, special aptitudes and interests, health information or others. For knowledge of tests of this nature, consult with the Research and Guidance Coordinator.

GENERAL INDEX

Achievement expectancy, 29

Achievement tests, defined, 18; available, 236

Adjustment, personal-social, 115; program for specially promoted pupils, 88

Administrative organization, of guidance, 12, 222; responsibility for guidance program, 68

Adolescence, characteristics and needs of, 3

Age-grade analysis form, use of, 32; sample, 231

Age-grade relationships, 85

American Democracy, purposes of education in, 2

Anecdotal records, 208

Appraisal of guidance program, 193

Aptitude tests, defined, 18

Audio-visual aids, 159

Authority, line and staff, 222

Authors, 210 ff

Autobiography, 47, 208

Basic needs, 109; of youth, 9

Career day, 147, 188

Case study, defined, 57; procedures for making, 58

Checklist, guidance services, 195

Class record sheet, 31

Clinical study, basis for special promotion, 87

Chronological age, definition of, 26

College entrance requirements, 135

Colleges and Universities, California, 137

Community organizations and agencies, 190

Counseling, defined, 123; educational, 128; suggestions for, 124; techniques of, 126; vocational, 145

Counselors, duties of, 78; qualifications of, 80

Cumulative record system, 62; cautions in initiating, 66; importance of, 63; record forms, 64

Curricula, adapting to meet individual differences, 92; individualizing curricular offerings, 90;

improvement through guidance data, 90

Deviation, definition of, 29

Differences, individual, 9

Economic efficiency, 10

Education, purposes of, 2

Educational guidance, defined, 128; making it effective, 130

Elective courses, 130

Evaluation, of guidance program, 206

Exceptional students, placement of, 86

Expectancy achievement, 29

Facilities for guidance, 72

Folder, cumulative record, 64

Girls, growth cycle, 6

Grade placement, 28

Graduation requirements, 134

Group guidance, 94

Growth, mental, 8; physical, 4; social and emotional, 8

Growth of boys and girls, 5, 7

Guidance data, collection of, 16; recording of, 62; uses of, 13, 83, 90, 95, 106

Guidance personnel, functions of, 78, growth of, 14; preparation of, 77; qualifications of, 80; recommended experience, 80

Guidance program, appraisal of, 193; essential characteristics of, 11; evaluation of, 15, 193; interpretation of, 183; list of services, 195; organization of, 12, 222; purposes of, 11; relation to community organizations, 69, 190; see also techniques; see also testing program

Guidance services, available from county office (Los Angeles), 35; checklist, 195

Hand-scored tests, 22

Health guidance, mental, 102, 109; physical, 103

High school students' problems, 125

Individual counseling, 123; see also counseling

Individual differences, 9; in curriculum adjustments, 92

245

7875

3